GROWING

Like Jesus

Essential Christian Concepts
for Elementary Students

GROWING
Like Jesus

Essential Christian Concepts
for Elementary Students

52 Versatile Lesson Plans

wph wesleyan
publishing
house

Indianapolis, Indiana

Copyright © 2005 by Wesleyan Publishing House
Published by Wesleyan Publishing House
Indianapolis, Indiana 46250
Printed in the United States of America

ISBN-13: 978-0-89827-290-1
ISBN-10: 0-89827-290-4

Written by Julia Roat-Abla and Colleen Derr.

Contents

How to Use This Book

The spiritual formation of children is a critical task that includes the development of their spirit, mind, relationships, and behavior—heart, head, hands, and habits. This book contains fifty-two versatile session plans to assist you in developing a child's *mind* by teaching basic truths of the Christian faith. To be successful in forming a child spiritually, instruction must be reinforced by modeled behavior and encouragement outside the teaching setting. These lessons are intended to be one part of a holistic approach to the discipleship of children. They are designed for use primarily as a supplement to existing discipleship curricula.

Here's how to make the most of this resource.

Step 1: Choose a Setting

Examine your church's overall children's ministry program and select the setting where this material will be most effective. Some possibilities for use are—

- Alongside existing Sunday school curriculum
- During the children's sermon portion of a worship service
- As one feature in a children's church program
- As the teaching material for a midweek children's program
- As the entire program of a specialized class devoted to discipleship

Step 2: Choose a Teaching Plan

Based on the setting that you have selected, determine how much time will be available for instruction. These session plans are versatile and offer teaching options ranging from five minutes to one hour. Based on the available time for instruction, choose one of four teaching options.

Option 1: 5-Minute Sessions

Include these session elements:

- Say (3–5 minutes)
- Action Point (1–2 minutes)

Possible uses:

- Add-on element to Sunday school curriculum
- Children's sermon for a worship service

Option 2: 15-Minute Sessions

Include these session elements:

- Memory Verse (5 minutes)
- Say (5 minutes)
- Action Point (3 minutes)
- Prayer (2 minutes)

Possible uses:

- Add-on to existing Sunday school curriculum
- Teaching portion of a midweek children's program
- One element of a children's church program

Option 3: 30-Minute Sessions

Include these session elements:

- Memory Verse (5 minutes)
- Say (5 minutes)
- Action Point (3 minutes)
- One Activity Option (7–10 minutes)
- Prayer (5 minutes)
- Bridge (2 minutes)

Possible uses:

- Teaching portion of a midweek children's program
- Teaching portion of a children's church program
- Small group study
- Home school lesson

Option 4: 60-Minute Sessions

Sixty-minute sessions call for the use of all session elements as well as additional resources, many of which are included in this book. In addition, some session elements are suggested here which do not appear in each printed session plan.

Use this suggested structure for a 60-minute session.

- Sharing Time—Build relationships by sharing life experiences that relate to the session content. (5–10 minutes)
- Worship Songs—See Music Resources section (page 121) for suggestions (10 minutes)
- Memory Verse (5–10 minutes)
- Say (5 minutes)
- Action Point (3 minutes)

- Activities (15–25 minutes)
- Prayer—See How To Teach Children to Pray section (page 125) for varied approaches (10 minutes)
- Bridge (2 minutes)

Possible uses:

- Midweek children's program
- Children's church program
- Small group study
- Catechism class

Step 3: Conduct an Assessment

Use the Assessment Tool to determine the knowledge base of your children. The tool will reveal which concepts the students already grasp and which need to be reinforced.

Step 4: Create a Teaching Calendar

Use the Teaching Calendar (page 144) to plan your activities for the quarter or year, including the concepts to be taught, session elements to include, activity options selected, and teaching tools to be used.

Step 5: Prepare to Teach

Become familiar with the elements of these sessions and spend adequate time preparing to communicate the biblical concept. There is room for lesson notes in the gray sidebar of each page.

- *Concept*—the Biblical truth to be communicated.
- *Memory Verse*—a variety of memorization activities are included in this book.
- *Before You Begin*—pre-session preparation suggestions.
- *Teaching Points*—primary points to emphasize during the session
- *Say*—a five-minute presentation of the biblical concept, intended to be either read aloud or summarized during the session
- *Activities Options*—student activities that may be used during the session to reinforce the concept experientially.
- *Action Point*—a question, challenge, or suggested action to assist children in applying the concept to life.
- *Prayer*—a suggested prayer to assist the leader in verbalizing our response to God's truth.
- *Bridge*—a statement, intended to be read aloud or summarized, that arouses interest in the next session.

Also become familiar with the additional resources provided in this book and plan ways to use them during the teaching sessions. Additional elements are—

- *Learning Concepts*—a listing of the fifty-two concepts presented in this book, arranged by topic (page 10).

- *Competency Goals for Elementary Students*—skills that children at this age level should be working toward mastering (page 11).

- *Developmental Characteristics of Elementary Students*—insights on how children learn and develop that will enhance your teaching and make it most beneficial to children (page 116).

- *Elementary Assessment Tool*—a pre-test to clarify the areas in which children need most intensive instruction. This tool may be used informally in one-to-one conversation or in a group setting. It also serves as a post-test to evaluate learning (page 119).

- *Elementary Scripture Memory Ideas*—a variety of ideas to help teach Scripture verses to preschool children (page 122).

- *How to Lead a Child to Christ*—a basic, step-by-step approach to leading a child to Christ (page 124).

- *How to Teach Children to Pray*—a variety of methods for introducing children to prayer (page 126).

- *Music Resources*—a list of age-appropriate worship music options (page 128).

- *Additional Resources*—a list of tools to assist in teaching children and organizing children's ministry (page 129).

- *Reproducible Activity Items*—supplemental items provided for some lessons (page 131).

- *Teaching Calendar*—a tool for developing a teaching plan and tracking progress (page 144).

Step 6: Assess Learning

After completing the teaching cycle, reassess the children's knowledge using the assessment tool. Identify areas that may need to be revisited and reviewed.

Teaching Tips

- Understand the biblical concepts. It is vital to spend time in prayer, Bible study, and preparation for each lesson. Read the recommended scriptures and reach a solid understanding of each truth.

- Understand your students. In order to effectively communicate these concepts and to take advantage of the most appropriate teaching tools, it is vital to understand where children are developmentally. Get to know your students so that you can communicate God's truth to them.

Learning Concepts

God

1. There is only one God.
2. God is greater than anything.
3. God made the world from nothing.
4. God cares about all people.
5. God is perfect, fair, and faithful.
6. God is everywhere all the time.
7. God is all-knowing.
8. God is all-powerful.
9. We talk with God through prayer.
10. God wants us to worship and praise Him.

Scripture

11. The Bible is God's Word.
12. The Bible shows us who God is and what He has done.
13. God's Word never changes.
14. The Bible tells us how to live.

Self

15. I am created in the image of God.
16. I am unique and valuable to God.
17. I am responsible for my choices.
18. God wants my thoughts and actions to be pure.
19. I can use my talents and abilities to please God.

Jesus

20. Jesus is the Son of God.
21. Jesus lived on earth.
22. Jesus is both God and human.
23. Jesus was tempted but did not sin.
24. Jesus came to be our savior.
25. Jesus died on the cross.
26. God raised Jesus from the dead.

Salvation

27. All people have done wrong.
28. Sin separates people from God.
29. God loves us even though we have sinned.
30. God sent his son to forgive our sins.
31. Jesus died to forgive my sin.
32. God forgives those who believe in Jesus.
33. We are adopted into God's family by faith.
34. We can live forever in heaven.

The Church

35. The Church is all believers everywhere.
36. We belong to a local church.
37. Baptism represents our new life in Christ.
38. The Lord's Supper represents Christ's sacrifice.
39. We serve others by helping at church.
40. We support the church with our tithes.
41. The Church spreads the gospel around the world.
42. Christians pray for one another.
43. Christians meet together for worship.

The Christian Life

44. God sent the Holy Spirit to help us.
45. The Holy Spirit helps us understand the truth.
46. The Holy Spirit helps us obey God.
47. The Holy Spirit helps us serve others.
48. We grow stronger by learning God's Word.
49. We grow stronger by praying to God.
50. Christians help those in need.
51. Living for Jesus makes life better.
52. Jesus will come back and take us to heaven.

Competency Goals for Elementary Students

Elementary Students Can . . .

1. Locate a Bible passage by book, chapter and verse.

2. Recite the books of the New Testament.

3. Read the Bible and apply it to their lives.

4. Pray for others and themselves.

5. Recite the Ten Commandments and the Lord's Prayer.

6. Tell friends about Jesus.

7. Trust God to answer prayer.

8. Participate in worship.

God

Memory Verse

Hear O Israel: The Lord our God,
the Lord is one. Deuteronomy 6:4

1 There is only one God.

Before You Begin

- Read Genesis 12, Isaiah 44:6, and Hebrews 12.
- Review the Teaching Points to familiarize yourself with the ideas to emphasize in this session.
- Read the session plan and select the elements that you will include.
- Choose a Bible memorization technique from those listed on page 122. Be sure to vary your teaching technique from session to session.
- If you choose to include a learning activity, gather the materials you will need.
  - For Activity 1 you will need a basket with examples of some things that people commonly worship, including examples of time (a watch), money (some coins or bills), possessions (a matchbox car), other people (a picture of movie star), sports (a baseball), and others.
  - For Activity 2 you will need copies of the worksheet found on page 132 for each student.

Teaching Points

- There is only one God.
- There are no other gods.
- God wants us to put Him first in our life.

Say

Long ago many people worshipped many gods. Even today, some cultures still worship more than one god. But the first thing God wanted people like Abraham, Moses, and David to know was that He is the only God that they should worship. No other gods, such as Baal, Zeus, or Thor, would do. They weren't alive. They were usually carved out of stone or wood. People thought that if their crops failed or the weather was bad it was because their gods were upset over something. But God told His people—and that includes you and me—that He alone created the universe and that He alone should be worshipped. There is only one God.

It's important to think about what we may be worshiping, for there are many ways that we can put other things before God. We may not believe in stone or wooden gods, but sometimes it's easy to put ourselves or what we want ahead of God. Maybe the newest gaming system or other things we own are more important than God to us. Maybe our wants come before something God wants. Perhaps we spend all our money on ourselves rather than contributing to a church relief project.

God created us and He loves us. He wants us to put Him first in our lives.

Activity Options

Activity 1: *Our idols.* Even though we don't worship gods made of stone or wood, we can put other things before God. Bring a basket of objects that people today worship, including examples of time (a watch), money (some coins or bills), possessions (a matchbox car), other people (a picture of movie star), sports (a baseball), and others. Discuss how people worship these things. How should we treat those things if we really live as if there is only one God?

Activity 2: *Comes down to one.* There are a lot of numbers in the Bible. This worksheet found on page 132 reminds students that all these numbers come down to the *one* God we serve.

Action Point

Do you ever treat God like He is secondary in your life by your attitude or the way you treat other people? What are some ways you can put God first at school? At home? When you play? In everything you do, remember there is only one God.

Prayer

Lord, we believe that You are the only true God. Help us today to put You first in our lives. We want to learn more about You so that we may know how to love You more. Amen.

For Next Time

Today we talked about the fact that we serve only one God. Next week we'll discover why.

God

2 God is greater than anything.

Before You Begin

- Read Deuteronomy 6:5, Psalm 135, and Psalm 147:5.
- Review the Teaching Points to familiarize yourself with the ideas to emphasize in this session.
- Read the session plan and select the elements that you will include.
- Choose a Bible memorization technique from those listed on page 122. Be sure to vary your teaching technique from session to session.
- If you choose to include a learning activity, gather the materials you will need.
  - For Activity 2 you will need glow-in-the-dark stars and planets, a hot glue gun, fishing line, small pieces of the rough side of Velcro™ (to attach to underside of the stars), and small flashlights.

Teaching Points

- God is greater than anything.
- God created everything.
- God is greater than the things He created.
- We worship God because He alone is worthy.

Say

There's nothing that compares to our God. We serve a God who is far beyond anything we could think of or even understand. Because God created everything, He's greater than His creation—and this includes the mountains, the oceans, the planets, the sun, the galaxy, and even the universe. These are things we know are big. Some things are even light years away and millions of miles long. But these are tiny compared to God because He is greater than anything.

We also know God is greater than His creation because He has existed forever—He is eternal. It's hard for us to imagine that God lived before there was even time, but He gave us time. We can measure how long

14

ago the dinosaurs walked the earth, how quickly recess is over, or how soon it will be until dinner. But God is greater than time because He does not have a beginning or an end. God is greater than anything.

Sometimes we talk and sing about how great God is. We may feel amazed or awestruck at those times. But this is one very important reason why we worship him. There's nothing and no one greater than our God.

Activity Options

Activity 1: *Which is greater?* Ask the students to stand in a line in the middle of the classroom. Give them two options, and ask them to choose which is greater by moving to one side of the classroom if they vote for the first choice and to the opposite side of the classroom if they vote for the second. Use things that may be chosen based on opinion. For example, give options such as Coke or Pepsi, baseball or basketball, and the ocean or the mountains.

Finally, finish with choices they can all agree on, such as the President of the United States or God, and a billion dollars or God. At the end of the game, emphasize once again that God is greater than everything.

Activity 2: *Impromptu planetarium.* Attach glow in the dark stars and planets to the walls of your classroom, hang some from the ceiling with hot glue and fishing line, and attach some stars to the carpet with the rough side of Velcro™. Turn off the lights and give the students flashlights so that when they enter the room it looks like they just stepped into space. As you observe the stars, emphasize once again that God is greater than all the stars, planets, and even the entire universe.

Action Point

We worship God because He alone is worthy. You can thank and praise God that He is greater than any trouble or concern you might have.

Prayer

Dear God, even though You are so great, we thank You for loving us and creating us. Help us to understand how great Your love for us is. Amen.

For Next Time

Have you ever created something from nothing? This may be impossible for us to do, but next week we'll learn that God can.

God

Memory Verse
In the beginning
God created the heavens
and the earth. Genesis 1:1

3 God made the world from nothing.

Before You Begin

■ Read Genesis 2, Isaiah 40:28, and Hebrews 11:3.
■ Review the Teaching Points to familiarize yourself with the ideas to emphasize in this session.
■ Read the session plan and select the elements that you will include.
■ Choose a Bible memorization technique from those listed on page 122. Be sure to vary your teaching technique from session to session.
■ If you choose to include a learning activity, gather the materials you will need.
  • For Activity 1 you will need many different objects made out of a variety of materials such as metal, wood, stone, paper, and plastic. You may choose to include things such as wire, toothpicks, rubber bands, straws, gravel, sequins, or pipe cleaners. You will also need a strong adhesive or a hot glue gun.
  • For Activity 2 you will need Play-Doh™ or modeling clay in a variety of colors.

Teaching Points

■ God existed before creation.
■ God made the world from nothing.
■ God created the world by speaking it into existence.

Say

How many of you have seen a magic trick where something appears out of nowhere? We often ask, "How did they do that?" But we know that these "tricks" are illusions that fool the eye. Everything comes from something.

Everything we as humans create begins as something else. If you want to build a house, you need bricks, wood, and other materials to put it together. And this is true even with ideas. Thomas Edison invented the light bulb. But he had to make hundreds of bulbs that didn't work before he knew how to create the one that did. He used his past experiences and prior knowledge of physics and chemistry to discover how glass, metal, and gases could produce a new creation that gives us light.

But the Bible begins with our God creating something out of absolutely nothing. Last week we talked about how great our God is. He is so great that He has no beginning and no end. In fact, God existed before creation. And when He imagined a creation that He could love, it came into existence. God did not use an illusion to make the world appear.

And He didn't have to give it several tries before He got it right. God decided His creation was good the first time. That tells you how great God is, doesn't it?

Activity Options

Activity 1: *Junk sculpture.* Ask students to create a sculpture of an animal or object, but don't give them any materials. After they complain that they can't make something from nothing, give them a variety of small objects to create their sculpture. Remind them that in order to create something, they had to start with something, but God can make something from nothing.

Activity 2: *Creative hands.* Give the children a piece of clay to sculpt as you talk about the lesson. As they finish their sculptures, remind them that in order for us to create anything we must begin with something else, like the clay they've been using.

Action Point

Appreciate God's greatness this week as you are surrounded by all that He made out of nothing.

Prayer

God, we are amazed when we look at Your creation that you created something so amazing out of nothing. Help us to be thankful for such a beautiful and creative world. Amen.

For Next Time

When God created the universe, He designed it with care and love. Next week, we'll learn about something else that God loves and cares for.

God

Memory Verse

For God so loved the world that he gave his one and only Son, that whoever believes in him shall not perish but have eternal life. John 3:16

4 God cares about all people.

Before You Begin

- Read Psalm 55:22, Matthew 6:25–34, 1 Peter 5:7, and 1 John 4:9–10.
- Review the Teaching Points to familiarize yourself with the ideas to emphasize in this session.
- Read the session plan and select the elements that you will include.
- Choose a Bible memorization technique from those listed on page 122. Be sure to vary your teaching technique from session to session.
- If you choose to include a learning activity, gather the materials you will need.
  - For Activity 1 you will need magazines, poster board, glue, and scissors.
  - For Activity 2 determine a location for clean-up, if away from church get prior parental permission. Gloves and garbage bags are needed for this activity.

Teaching Points

- God loves all His creation.
- God thinks and feels and has a name.
- God created us to love Him and others.
- God wants to take care of His creation.

Say

Have you ever made something that was later broken? How did it make you feel to see something you created destroyed?

Imagine how God, as great as He is, might feel about what He has made. God loves everyone no matter what shape, size, or color they are. Why? First of all, He loves us because He made us. Just like we care for the things we create, God enjoys and wants to protect what He has made. God cares about all people.

Because He loves His creation, He is happy when we take care of the earth and other people. He is sad when the things in His creation are broken or hurting. And when we, His children, are feeling broken or hurting, He wants us to come to Him for comfort and repair—even if we are hurting because we have messed up. Only God can make us whole. God cares about all people.

Activity Options

Activity 1: *Collage poster*. Have students use old magazines to find as many different kinds of people as possible. Use the pictures to create a collage on a poster board with John 3:16 in the center.

Activity 2: *Creation Clean-Up.* Select a location near the church that would benefit from a clean up. Take garbage bags, gloves & students and pick up trash. Remind students how important it is that we take care of God's creation.

Action Point

Just as God loves and values all people, we should love and value all people, even if they are different from us.

Prayer

Dear God, You have told us and have shown us over and over again how much You care for us and for Your entire creation. Help us to protect and care for each other and for the world we live in. Amen.

For Next Time

This week we talked about God caring about His creation. Next week we'll learn more about His personality.

God

Memory Verse

The Lord is gracious and compassionate,
slow to anger and rich in love. The Lord
is good to all; he has compassion on
all he has made. Psalm 145:8–9

5 — God is perfect, fair, and faithful.

Before You Begin

- Read Deuteronomy 32:4, Psalm 18:30, Psalm 100:5, Isaiah 6:3, and 1 John 4:7–8.
- Review the Teaching Points to familiarize yourself with the ideas to emphasize in this session.
- Read the session plan and select the elements that you will include.
- Choose a Bible memorization technique from those listed on page 122. Be sure to vary your teaching technique from session to session.
- If you choose to include a learning activity, gather the materials you will need.
  - For Activity 1 you will need paper and pencils for each student.
  - For Activity 2 you will need paper and pencils for each student.

Teaching Points

- God's goodness is reflected in His holiness and love working together.
- God is perfect.
- God is fair.
- God is faithful.

Say

When you think about God, what kind of expression does He have on His face? Many people think God has an angry face when we mess up. Some people think God looks bored and couldn't care less. Other people think God looks stern and spends all of His time creating a long list of demands for us to obey.

While we know that God has thoughts and emotions like us, God is also completely good. His character is love and holiness. He can't be anything but good, loving, and holy.

We know God is good because He is perfect. God is also good because He is completely fair. God seeks justice for whatever is right. When there is a question, God sees and does the right thing.

Finally, God is always faithful. He does not say one thing and do another. We know that God keeps His promises. God is good, loving, and holy. He is also perfect, fair, and faithful.

Activity Options

Activity 1: *Faces*. Draw four smiley faces showing different emotions like joy, sadness, surprise, and anger. As you begin the lesson, show these faces and ask the children to name the emotions they reflect.

Activity 2: *Journaling*. Encourage children to write for five minutes using the following writing prompts: When you think about of God, what kind of expression does He have on His face? What do you think God looks like?

Action Point

Think about the kind of expression you imagined God having on His face before you came today. Now that we've talked about God's character, has the expression you imagined changed at all? Ask God to help you to think of Him in the right way—as a faithful and loving God.

Prayer

Lord, because you are so good to us, we thank You today. We pray that we might show Your grace and compassion as we learn to follow You. Amen.

For Next Time

We know of God's greatness because He loves us and knows us. But how can He love and know each of us all at the same time? Come next week to find out.

God

Memory Verse
Come near to God and he
will come near to you. James 4:8

6 God is everywhere all the time.

Before You Begin

- Read Psalm 139:7–10, Isaiah 57:15, and Acts 2.
- Review the Teaching Points to familiarize yourself with the ideas to emphasize in this session.
- Read the session plan and select the elements that you will include.
- Choose a Bible memorization technique from those listed on page 122. Be sure to vary your teaching technique from session to session.
- If you choose to include a learning activity, gather the materials you will need.
  - For Activity 1 you will take your students on a walk around the church grounds.
  - For Activity 2 you will need poster board, travel magazines, glue, and scissors. (Ask a local travel agent if they have any outdated travel magazines that you may have for free.)

Teaching Points

- God reveals himself in creation and history.
- God reveals himself in Scripture and in Jesus Christ.
- God is present and near to us all the time.

Say

Do you have to see something to know it's there? Although God is invisible, He shows himself to us in special ways. We call this "revelation." We can see God's hand in creation and in history. But we also know God has shown himself to us through the Bible, which gives us the wonderful story of His relationship with people. This story also tells us about the most important revelation of God: Jesus Christ. Jesus has returned to heaven, but He has sent His Spirit to be with us until he returns. Through the Holy Spirit, He is with us all the time.

Remember a few weeks ago when we talked about God being eternal? That means He is not bound by space or by time. God can be present and near to us all the time. When we gather to worship Him in church, He is with us, just like He is present in every Christian church around the world. When you pray to Him in your room at home, He is with you. When you hike up to the tallest point of a mountain, He's there. If you were to dive to the deepest underwater cave, He would be there. There's no way to escape the presence of God. He is always available. And He's always ready to talk to you. God is everywhere all the time.

Activity Options

Activity 1: *Can you see God.* Take your class on a walking tour around the church property. Have the students point out things in Creation that show us God (i.e. flowers, rocks, birds, air, etc...)

Activity 2: *Where is God?* Cut out pictures of travel destinations to attach to a poster. As you talk about each place make it special, remind your students that God is in each of the places in the pictures.

Action Point

As you go to different places this week—to school, your house, or a store—keep in mind that God is always with you.

Prayer

Lord, today we thank You for always being near to us. Help us now to have open eyes and listening hearts so we may be aware of Your presence. Amen.

For Next Time

God is not only near to us, but He also knows everything about us. Next week we'll discover what His incredible knowledge and wisdom mean for us.

God

7 God is all-knowing.

Before You Begin

- Read 1 Chronicles 28:9, Psalm 139:1–4, Isaiah 55:8–9, and Hebrews 4:13.
- Review the Teaching Points to familiarize yourself with the ideas to emphasize in this session.
- Read the session plan and select the elements that you will include.
- Choose a Bible memorization technique from those listed on page 122. Be sure to vary your teaching technique from session to session.
- If you choose to include a learning activity, gather the materials you will need.
  - For Activity 1 you will need several encyclopedias.
  - For Activity 2 you will need copies of the choral reading based on Psalm 139 found on page 133 for each student.

Teaching Points

- God has unsurpassing knowledge.
- God is wise in His understanding and knowledge.
- God knows me.
- God is all-knowing.

Say

Have you ever wished that you could know everything there is to know? Maybe you've wished for that kind of knowledge right before you've taken a test at school or when someone has asked you a tough question. But no one can know everything. You could search the entire Internet and not find everything you can know. The Library of Congress in Washington, D.C. has 530 miles of book-shelves that hold 29 million books, nearly three million recordings, twelve million photographs and nearly four million maps. But even it does not contain all the knowledge in this world. Only God is all-knowing.

We've been talking about how God is good, loving, and always present. It probably won't surprise you that He is also very smart. God is aware of everything. We may not be able to do two things at the same time—at least not very well—but God sees and knows everything that happens. But there is more than just basic knowledge that makes God smart. He also understands how things work together, and what is best for each one of His children. Most importantly, though, is that our God, who is always present and always near, also knows everything about us. God is all-knowing.

Activity Options

Activity 1: *Encyclopedia*. Bring in several volumes from an encyclopedia set and allow the children to look at them for several minutes to get an idea of the vast amount of knowledge that exists in the world. Let each student find an interesting and new fact to share. Emphasize that God knows all that is in the encyclopedias and much, much more.

Activity 2: *Choral reading from Psalm 139.* Provide copies of the choral reading found on page 133 for each of the students, and read it aloud together. Ask how the poem makes them feel? What does the poem say about God?

Action Point

Are you dealing with a difficult problem? Ask God to share His wisdom with you and guide you in the right direction.

Prayer

Lord, Your knowledge and wisdom are beyond our understanding. Search our thoughts and our hearts, and give us Your wisdom as we seek to do Your will. Amen.

For Next Time

You shouldn't be surprised that God, our creator, is very powerful. But His mighty power is sometimes shown in some unexpected ways. Next week we'll talk about what God's power means to our relationship with Him.

God

Memory Verse

For since the creation of the world God's invisible qualities—his eternal power and divine nature—have been clearly seen, being understood from what has been made, so that men are without excuse. Romans 1:20

8 God is all powerful.

Before You Begin

- Read Psalm 66:1–7, Ephesians 6:10, and Ephesians 1:15–23.
- Review the Teaching Points to familiarize yourself with the ideas to emphasize in this session.
- Read the session plan and select the elements that you will include.
- Choose a Bible memorization technique from those listed on page 122. Be sure to vary your teaching technique from session to session.
- If you choose to include a learning activity, gather the materials you will need.
  - For Activity 1 you will need pictures or action figures of superheroes, such as Superman, Spiderman, or Batman.

Teaching Points

- God is all powerful.
- God's power is shown by His goodness and love.
- God helps us to be what He wants us to be.

Say

In many cartoons or movies, people look to a superhero for help. When they are good, like Superman or Spiderman, they have special powers that they use to help people. Superman can see through concrete. Spiderman can swing from building to building. This kind of power that you see on cartoons or in films is limited.

But God's power has no limit. There is nothing—not even Kryptonite—that can stop God's power.

His power is sometimes compared to the crashing waves or lightening and thunder. Although God is powerful, He always has our best interests in mind. His power is never harsh or hurtful to us. God's power is shown by His goodness and love. He has the power to be God. He is able to do whatever He wills. And thankfully, God is good, loving, and full of knowledge.

God's power is like the influence that some people have on you—people whom you would go to for advice. For example, your dad or your grandma may have a lot of power over you because you listen to what they say. When we allow God's mighty power to work in our lives, we will find that we will be influenced to act more like He would act—in good and loving ways. His power helps us to be who He wants us to be.

Activity Options

Activity 1: *Super powers.* Show the children pictures of super heroes or action figures and discuss the specific powers that each one possesses. These characters are all ideas of what the world considers powerful. Emphasize that God's power is much more amazing.

Activity 2. *Everyday Superheroes.* God's power is shown in His goodness and His love. Ask your students to discuss ways that they could show the influence of God's power in their lives this week. Remind them that God's power in our lives motivates us to love and help others. And by helping others, they, too, can be superheroes. Have children write down one thing they'll do this week to help someone else.

Action Point

Do you feel powerless when you think about a certain circumstance in your life? God is powerful enough to help you with it. Ask Him for help.

Prayer

Lord, we thank You today that Your power is shown in Your goodness and Your love. Help us each day to love You and to love each other. Amen.

For Next Time

We can see God's power and His influence in our lives the more we talk to Him. Next week we'll talk about how we can communicate with God.

God

Memory Verse

Here I am! I stand at the door and knock. If anyone hears my voice and opens the door, I will come in and eat with him, and he with me. Revelation 3:20

9 We talk with God through prayer.

Before You Begin

- Read 2 Chronicles 7:14, Psalm 17:1, Isaiah 65:24, and Matthew 6:9–13.
- Review the Teaching Points to familiarize yourself with the ideas to emphasize in this session.
- Read the session plan and select the elements that you will include.
- Choose a Bible memorization technique from those listed on page 122. Be sure to vary your teaching technique from session to session.
- If you choose to include a learning activity, gather the materials you will need.
  - In Activity 1 you will need a small bowl or incense burner, incense, and matches.
  - In Activity 2 you will need poster board, hole punch, craft supplies and markers.

Teaching Points

- We can have a relationship with God.
- Relationships depend on good communication.
- We talk with God through prayer.

Say

What are some of the ways we communicate with people today? You might use a cell phone, e-mail, talking, sign language, or facial expressions. But God has given us a special way to communicate with Him.

God created us because He is love. He wants to have a relationship with us, and one of the most important things in a good relationship is good communication. Think about your best friend. How often do you talk? What would happen if you stopped talking to him or her? If you don't communicate, you don't have much of a relationship.

God, more than any friend, wants to know what's going on with you, and He wants you to tell Him. We call it prayer. But because of who God is, there is a special way we pray. Often prayer seems hard to do, but there are four simple steps that can help us talk to God. They spell "A-C-T-S."

Begin with A-doration by simply praising God for who He is: good, kind, loving, powerful, and near to us. Then in C-onfession, we tell God what we have done wrong, things that are unloving and not how God created us to be. In T-hanksgiving we thank God for the good things He's given to us. Finally, with S-upplication we ask God for help with the things that concern us.

The best thing about prayer, however, is that God has something to say to us. Sometimes, all we need to do is quiet our minds and our hearts and listen. How amazing it is that we can talk with God through prayer!

Activity Options

Activity 1: *Our rising prayers.* In Scripture, the prayers of faithful people were sometimes pictured as the smell of perfumed incense rising to heaven. Illustrate this by having incense burning as students enter your classroom. Pray together as a class using "A-C-T-S" or another idea from "How to Teach Children to Pray," found on page 126.

Activity 2: *A-C-T-S of prayer.* Have students write down the acrostic of A-C-T-S (Adoration, Confession, Thanksgiving, Supplication) to keep in their Bible as a reminder of the elements of prayer. Cut poster board into bookmark size one for each student. Provide craft items to decorate and ribbon to tie to the top.

Action Point

God the best friend you could ever have. Take time this week to talk to Him through prayer.

Prayer

Lord, we thank You for the opportunity we have through prayer to talk with You. Help us to meet with You often and get to know You more. Amen.

For Next Time

This week we've learned that prayer is talking with God. Often when we pray, we thank Him for things He has done. Next week we'll learn about another way we can communicate our praise to God.

God

Memory Verse

Worship the Lord with gladness; come before him with joyful songs. Psalm 100:2

10 God wants us to praise and worship Him.

Before You Begin

- Read Deuteronomy 6:6, Psalm 47:7–8, Matthew 4:10, and Romans 12.
- Review the Teaching Points to familiarize yourself with the ideas to emphasize in this session.
- Read the session plan and select the elements that you will include.
- Choose a Bible memorization technique from those listed on page 122. Be sure to vary your teaching technique from session to session.
- If you choose to include a learning activity, gather the materials you will need.
  - For Activity 2 you will need copies of the worksheet found on page 134 for each student.

Teaching Points

- Worship is all about God and not about us.
- God wants us to praise and worship Him.
- We worship God by giving Him our whole life and by loving others.

Say

We know that communicating with God is important for us to have a good relationship with Him. Prayer is our basic communication with God. We can pray by ourselves, but often we gather together with other people and pray together. Worship is like a longer, bigger prayer where sometimes we say something to God and sometimes God says something to us.

Our worship of God begins with focusing on Him. We can talk about His greatness, His holiness, His love, and His power. In fact, the worship services are centered around God's people preparing, listening, and responding to His words.

It's important to know and understand what God is saying to us, and sometimes it helps when there's more than one person listening. You can probably name some of the things we do in worship to hear what God has to say. First, we gather together and prepare our hearts through prayer and singing. Then we actually hear God's Word! We may join in a Scripture reading or we may listen to the pastor preach a sermon. Finally, we respond to what God has said. This may mean taking communion, singing, praying, or giving our offerings.

Worship can be full of praise and energy or it can be very contemplative and awe-inspiring. But our best and most worshipful response is to offer ourselves to God in response to His love for us. God wants us to praise and worship Him.

Activity Options

Activity 1: *Statements of worship*. Model a statement of worship for the children. For example, you might say, "God, you make the most beautiful trees," or, "God, you've formed the most incredible mountains! Ask the students to take turns making their own worship statements.

Activity 2: *Worship word bank*. Hand out the worksheet found on page 134 to the students. Have them match the Scripture references to the words that describe various elements of worship.

Action Point

Worship has many forms. How can you worship God in a new way this week?

Prayer

Lord, we thank You and praise You for who You are—mighty and powerful, loving and kind. We offer these gifts of thanksgiving and praise as we worship You. Amen.

For Next Time

God speaks to us through prayer and worship, but He also communicates to us through the Bible. Next week we'll learn more about what God wants to tell us through Scripture.

Scripture

11 The Bible is God's Word.

Before You Begin

■ Read 1 Timothy 4:13, 2 Timothy 3:16, and 2 Peter 1:20–21,
■ Review the Teaching Points to familiarize yourself with the ideas to emphasize in this session.
■ Read the session plan and select the elements that you will include.
■ Choose a Bible memorization technique from those listed on page 122. Be sure to vary your teaching technique from session to session.
■ If you choose to include a learning activity, gather the materials you will need.
   • For Activity 1 you will need a variety of Bibles—different translations, sizes, and languages (if available).
   • For Activity 2 you will need five sheets of paper, a sheet of cardstock, and pencils for each student.

Teaching Points

■ God speaks to us through the Bible.
■ The Bible is God's Word because it points to Jesus.
■ The written Word helps us spread the good news to everyone.

Say

Here's an amazing fact: the Bible has been translated into 2,018 different languages! It took over 1,500 years to be written, and it's the best selling book of all time. This must be an important book!

The Bible is important because it gives us the story of God in written form. The Bible is God's written Word.

God certainly has a lot to say to us. He wants us to know what kind of God He is—a creating, loving, powerful God who wants to talk with us. To make sure we understand who He is, God gave us His words in written form. Many people, like Moses, Daniel, Luke, and John wrote about their relationship with God and how He spoke to them. But He still speaks to us today through His written Word. In the Bible, we read a story that begins with creation and ends with God coming to His creation. It is a story of God and His people, and most importantly, the greatest expression of His love—Jesus Christ. We read and understand God's words because we are a part of that story. And because God's words are written down, we have the ability to share God's story with others around the world. The Bible is truly a great gift from God!

Activity Options

Activity 1: *The Bible*. Bring a variety of Bibles to class so the students can pass them around and compare them. Use Bibles of different translations, sizes, and languages (if available). Take time to show the students the different parts of the Bible. Have them find these things together: Table of Contents, Old and New Testaments, Books of the Bible-Read them aloud together, Chapters and Verses. Find the memory verse and read together.

Activity 2: *God's Story/My Story*. Create a book by folding 5 sheets of paper and a sheet of cardstock in half and stapling them along the fold. Have the children write down a story from the Bible in their own words in the first half of their book, and in the second half, have them write down their testimony. When they are finished, remind them that both stories relate to God; they are a part of the story that God is writing.

Action Point

God wants to teach you about himself through the Bible. Make a commitment this week to read your Bible so you can learn more about God's story.

Prayer

Lord, we thank You that You have given us the Bible, and that through it, we can learn more about You and Your story. Help us today to use your Word to grow in the faith and to tell others about You. Amen.

For Next Time

What is so important about God's written Word? Next week we will discover what is in Scripture that makes it so important to us.

Scripture

12 The Bible shows us who God is and what He has done.

Before You Begin

- Read Exodus 17:14, Psalm 78:1–8, John 5:39, and 2 Timothy 3:14–15.
- Review the Teaching Points to familiarize yourself with the ideas to emphasize in this session.
- Read the session plan and select the elements that you will include.
- Choose a Bible memorization technique from those listed on page 122. Be sure to vary your teaching technique from session to session.
- If you choose to include a learning activity, gather the materials you will need.

For Activity 1 you will need a family scrapbook or photo album that displays pictures from a family vacation.

For Activity 2 you will need to ask someone in your church (preferably an elderly person) to give his or her testimony to the class.

Teaching Points

- The Bible is God's story—a story about how God loves His people.
- We read the Bible to learn about God and how we can be in a relationship with Him.
- We are a part of God's story, and we need to tell God's story to others.
- The Bible shows us who God is and what He has done.

Say

Everybody likes to hear a good story. It can be funny or sad, scary or exciting. Some of the best stories are a little bit of both. From the beginning of our part in God's story, He has inspired men to record His great deeds and His interaction with the creation He loves.

It's kind of like a giant old family scrapbook. In a scrapbook, you'll find photographs and memories of past holidays, special occasions, vacations, or reunions. The pictures and stories on each page spark memories of who we are as a family and how important our relationships with one another are. The events are recorded for people to remember and to pass on to their children.

Scripture holds pictures and stories that also help us to remember how important and valuable we are to God. In the Bible, there are amazing stories like the one in which Jesus feeds five thousand people with a small basket of loaves and fish. But there are also scary stories like the one about Paul being shipwrecked. All these stories were written down to show others who God is and how we can have a relationship with Him. That's the reason Scripture was first written, beginning with Moses and the prophets many years ago. They wrote down the words and actions of God so future generations could know more about God's character. The Bible shows us who God is and what He has done.

Activity Options

Activity 1: *Scrapbook.* Bring a scrapbook or photo album showing family holidays or vacations. Compare your scrapbook to the Bible, emphasizing that Scripture is like God's scrapbook.

Activity 2: *Living Testimony.* Invite an older member of your church to come to the class and give their testimony. Allow time for questions. You may want to prepare a few questions about their story before class to help prompt discussion.

Action Point

Everyone loves to tell stories. What stories do you know from the Bible? Could you tell them to someone who has never heard them?

Prayer

Lord, thank You for inviting us into Your story. As we read about Your love for us, help us to share Your story with others. Amen.

For Next Time

The Bible has been around for a very long time. How much longer do you think God's Word will last? We'll find out next week.

Scripture

13 God's Word never changes.

Before You Begin

- Read Psalm 12:6, Psalm 119:11, Matthew 24:35, and John 1:1.
- Review the Teaching Points to familiarize yourself with the ideas to emphasize in this session.
- Read the session plan and select the elements that you will include.
- Choose a Bible memorization technique from those listed on page 122. Be sure to vary your teaching technique from session to session.
- If you choose to include a learning activity, gather the materials you will need.
  - For Activity 1 you will need one of your favorite things, particularly something that has become worn out over time.

Teaching Points

- God's revelation in written word has been passed down to us.
- When God's Word is hidden in our heart, it endures; it never changes.
- We are responsible for passing on words of life that we read in the Bible to others.

Say

The ancient Egyptians inscribed some words on a stone in 196 B.C. We now call it the Rosetta Stone. It tells about a young king's royal decree in three different languages. When they wrote down the story, they hoped it would last forever; however, today, one of the languages is no longer used, and we only have a portion of the full decree because it has been broken and worn over time. Sadly, not even words inscribed into stone last forever.

We know that things don't last forever. Your favorite toy gets pretty banged up after you've played with it a lot. It gets dirty or torn. Depending on how much you use it, the more quickly it will wear out. Some things, like a dollar bill, wear out quickly because they're made of paper, while some wear down more slowly like the copper penny. But we know everything eventually wears out.

God's Word, however, is the exact opposite. The more we use it, the more it sticks in our heads and our hearts, which is one way God's Word endures. His Word also endures because it is written down. The Bible is a book that we can read over and over and over. We can sing it, memorize it, and hide it in our hearts. But hiding God's Word in our hearts doesn't mean keeping it to ourselves. God wants us to tell others what His Word says, and He also wants it to influence everything we say and do.

God's Word is eternal. It never changes. And as much as it is used, it will never decay or get worn out. God's Word will always be the same.

Activity Options

Activity 1: *A few of my favorite things.* Ask the class what their favorite toy is. How long have they had it? Is it still in the same condition as the day they first played with it? Why? After discussing some of their favorite toys, show the class one of your favorite things (something that you has become worn out after much use). End your discussion by telling the class that it is usually the things we love that wear out the quickest, but this is not true of God's Word. If we love it and put it to use, it will only endure.

Action Point

How do you hide God's Word in your heart? You can practice hiding His Word in your heart by memorizing, reading, or meditating on it often. Try one of these every day this week.

Prayer

Lord, help us to hide Your words in our hearts so they can grow and live in us, especially as we share these words of life with others. Amen.

For Next Time

God's written Word is full of stories that tell of what God has done and who He is. But these stories also teach us many things. Next week we will learn more about what the Bible can teach us so we can grow in our relationship with God.

Scripture

Memory Verse

All Scripture is God-breathed and is useful for teaching, rebuking, correcting and training in righteousness, so that the man of God may be thoroughly equipped for every good work. 2 Timothy 3:16–17

14 The Bible tells us how to live.

Before You Begin

- Read Psalm 119:9–24, Matthew 4:4, 2 Timothy 3:15, and James 1:22–25.
- Review the Teaching Points to familiarize yourself with the ideas to emphasize in this session.
- Read the session plan and select the elements that you will include.
- Choose a Bible memorization technique from those listed on page 122. Be sure to vary your teaching technique from session to session.
- If you choose to include a learning activity, gather the materials you will need.
  - For Activity 1 you will need an appliance instruction book and a Bible.

Teaching Points

- The Bible is a guide for life.
- The Old and New Testaments provide teaching for our lives.
- Scripture also gives us examples of how other faithful people lived.
- The Bible tells us how to live.

Say

Have you ever tried to put something together before reading the instructions? Often when we do this, the thing that we've put together doesn't work correctly. Or has one of your parents ever tried to find their way around a big city without a map or directions? Perhaps you ended up in the wrong place.

Scripture, or God's written Word, is kind of like an instruction book or a map for our lives. If we read it, we'll know the right ways to live, how to love God, and how to take care of His creation. People use the Bible to teach other people how to live for God. It gives us instructions and examples of how we should worship, pray, help, and love other people.

You'll definitely find instructions for many aspects of life in the Old Testament. One of the most important set of instructions is the Ten Commandments. But there are also directions in the New Testament like the Sermon on the Mount.

Thankfully, God doesn't just *tell* us how to live faithfully. He also shows us *how*. Scripture gives us many examples of faithful people who heard and followed God's Word. Their stories reveal God's love, forgiveness, and protection to all His people. The Bible is our guide for life; the Bible tells us how to live.

Activity Options

Activity 1: *Instruction book*. Bring an appliance instruction book. What are the chapters about? Is there a map? Does it have an index? Compare it to a Bible's books, chapters, concordance, maps, etc.

Activity 2: *Simon says*. Play the game Simon Says to emphasize the point of listening closely to directions.

Action Point

How has the Bible helped you grow in your relationship with God? What has it taught you about how you should relate to God and to other people?

Prayer

Lord, thank You for giving us these words of instruction and guidance as we follow You. Amen.

For Next Time

Did you ever wonder why God created people? Next week we'll talk about why and how God made us like He did.

Self

Memory Verse

So God created man in his own image, in the image of God he created him; male and female he created them. Genesis 1:27

15 I am created in the image of God.

Before You Begin

- Read Genesis 5:1, Acts 17:27–28, Galatians 3:28, and James 3:9.
- Review the Teaching Points to familiarize yourself with the ideas to emphasize in this session.
- Read the session plan and select the elements that you will include.
- Choose a Bible memorization technique from those listed on page 122. Be sure to vary your teaching technique from session to session.
- If you choose to include a learning activity, gather the materials you will need.
  - For Activity 1 you will need a small pet.
  - For Activity 2 you will need a digital or Polaroid™ camera, paper, and art supplies.

Teaching Points

- We are created in the image of God.
- God's image includes His character and qualities.
- We are the only part of God's creation that He made in His image.

Say

Has anyone ever told you, "You act just like your brother"? Or maybe someone has said, "I can see your mother in you." They were probably not only talking about similar physical features. They were more than likely also talking about your character traits. Perhaps you talk like your father or laugh like your mother.

Just like you may look and act like your mother, father, and other members of your family, you also have similar traits as God. The Bible says that we are all created in His image, meaning that we were created to be like Him.

For instance, humans are the only beings who have the ability to truly love, be creative, communicate in complex ways, and make moral choices. Your pet may be loyal and faithful, but it can't truly love like a human. It may choose to fetch a stick because it knows it will get a treat, not because it knows it's the right thing to do. Like God, we can see the difference between a good choice and a bad choice. And humans are the only creations with a sense of humor, so we can be sure that God likes to laugh. We alone love, make moral choices, and laugh because humans, not animals, reflect God's character and qualities.

Have you ever heard people say that older married couples start looking and acting like each other? Or have you ever heard someone call a child the "spitting image" of his or her parent. As we continue in our relationship with God, we are made more and more into His image.

Activity Options

Activity 1: *Pets.* Bring a small pet to class. Compare the pet to humans. Can the pet talk or write? Can the pet make moral decisions between right and wrong? Emphasize that God made us special, and He gave us character traits based on His image.

Activity 2: *In God's Image*. Using a Polaroid™ camera, take pictures of each student. Write today's memory verse in the center of a piece of poster board. Then tape the pictures of the students around the verse. As you place each child's picture on the poster, have the entire class say, "(Child's name) is made in the image of God!"

Action Point

Can you think of things you do that prove you are made in God's image? Thank God that He has given you characteristics that reflect himself.

Prayer

Lord, we thank You that You have made us in Your image. Teach us and help us to become more like You each day. Amen.

For Next Time

Next week, we will talk about how being made in God's image makes each one of us a very special part of His creation.

Self

Memory Verse
I praise you because I am fearfully and wonderfully made; your works are wonderful, I know that full well. Psalm 139:14

16 I am unique and valuable to God.

Before You Begin

- Read Psalm 139, John 15:16, Ephesians 1:4, and 1 Peter 5:7.
- Review the Teaching Points to familiarize yourself with the ideas to emphasize in this session.
- Read the session plan and select the elements that you will include.
- Choose a Bible memorization technique from those listed on page 122. Be sure to vary your teaching technique from session to session.
- If you choose to include a learning activity, gather the materials you will need.
  - For Activity 1 you will need four objects of your choosing. Three should be alike and one should be different.
  - For Activity 2 you will need something that has value to you—a piece of jewelry, an old Bible, or an antique. You may also choose to bring in pictures of things that people consider valuable—an expensive car, jewels, a beautiful mansion, or a famous painting.

Teaching Points

- Because we are made in God's image, we are very valuable to Him.
- God is our creator, and He is interested in each one of our lives.
- Because of our unique worth, God has given us special responsibilities.

Say

We often go through a lot of trouble to maintain and protect the things we consider valuable. We use safes, security systems, security cameras, bubble wrap, and padlocks just to keep things safe and sound. Cars, for example are expensive to buy and to keep up. They come with locks on the doors and windows. We take them to the car wash so the dirt doesn't scratch and rust the paint. We take the car to a mechanic for a tune-up so that it can run its best all the time.

God's relationship with us is very similar because we are unique and valuable to Him. He made us. And we are the only beings made in His image; we have thoughts, feelings, and responsibilities. Therefore, we have a unique worth. Even if you're a twin, a triplet, or a quadruplet, there is only *one* of you.

God knows each one of us personally, and He knows how different we are from everyone else. Because we are so valued, He has given us the special responsibility of caring for all of His creation and sharing His love with others. He wants us to be what He intended us to be—safe with Him. Isn't it awesome to know that you are unique, and that you are very valuable to God?

Activity Options

Activity 1: *Which one is not like the others?* Show the children the objects and ask them which one is not like the others. Remind them that though we are all created in the image of God, He also made each one of us unique.

Activity 2: *Valuable.* Show the children something that has value to you—a piece of jewelry, an old Bible, or an antique. You may also choose to bring in pictures of things that people consider valuable—an expensive car, jewels, a beautiful mansion, or a famous painting. Though all of these things have a great amount of value, each one of us has even more value to God.

Action Point

What is your most valued possession? How do you treat it? Because God treasures us even more so than you treasure your favorite things, how do you think we should treat each other?

Prayer

Lord, we thank You for creating each one of us as unique and valuable in Your sight. Help us to honor and love each other as a part of Your wondrous creation as well. Amen.

For Next Time

When God created us, He gave us each the freedom to make our own decisions. Next week we'll talk about making choices and the responsibility that comes with it.

Self

17 I am responsible for my choices.

Before You Begin

- Read Psalm 25:12, Luke 15:11–32, John 7:17, and John 14:15.
- Review the Teaching Points to familiarize yourself with the ideas to emphasize in this session.
- Read the session plan and select the elements that you will include.
- Choose a Bible memorization technique from those listed on page 122. Be sure to vary your teaching technique from session to session.
- If you choose to include a learning activity, gather the materials you will need.
  - For Activity 1 you will need paper and pencils for each student.

Teaching Points

- I am responsible for my choices.
- God has given us both the ability and the accountability of choice.
- We honor God by obeying Him and thinking of others.

Say

Don't you love the cereal aisle? There are so many delicious cereals like Captain Crunch, Froot Loops, Kix, Frosted Flakes, and Cookie Crunch. The cereal aisle proves that there are hundreds of choices that have to be made in a single day. Though choosing a cereal probably isn't the most important decision you make in a day, it is still one of many you may have to make. But there are many other choices we have to make each day, some of which are very important.

One of greatest things about being made in the image of God is the responsibility we have to make choices. There's really no other being that God created that makes decisions like we do. That's because choices are where our faith is put into action. God has given us the ability to choose between right and wrong and to follow Him when He says yes or no.

But He has not only given us the ability, He's also required the account-ability to make good choices. First, we have to live with the consequences of our decisions. If you decide to eat three bowls of Lucky Charms, you'll probably have to put up with a stomach ache later. More importantly, your decision to eat most of the cereal may leave everyone else hungry until lunch. It's important that when you make a choice to honor God, you think about others as well. Good choices honor both God and others. It's important to always remember that you are responsible for your choices.

Activity Options

Activity 1: *Choices.* Have the students make a list of all the choices they have already made that day—the time they got out of bed, the clothes they wore, what they ate for breakfast, etc.—to emphasize the amount of choices we make each day.

Activity 2: *Decisions.* Give the students a choice between two decisions. Some can be humorous, some serious, but consider options that involve honoring God and others.

Action Point

God has given us the ability to make choices, but we are also responsible for making good ones. Determine to make good choices this week.

Prayer

Lord, we thank You for giving us the freedom and ability to choose. Help us this day to choose You. Amen.

For Next Time

Perhaps one of the choices you made this week was to clean your room, take out the garbage, or to wash your clothes. Next week we'll talk about choosing to keep our thoughts and actions clean and pure.

Self

Memory Verse

Finally, brothers, whatever is true, whatever is noble, whatever is right, whatever is pure, whatever is lovely, whatever is admirable— if anything is excellent or praiseworthy—think about such things. Philippians 4:8

18 God wants my thoughts and actions to be pure.

Before You Begin

- Read Leviticus 11:44, Psalm 24:4–5, Proverbs 15:26, Matthew 5:8, and Ephesians 1:4.
- Review the Teaching Points to familiarize yourself with the ideas to emphasize in this session.
- Read the session plan and select the elements that you will include.
- Choose a Bible memorization technique from those listed on page 122. Be sure to vary your teaching technique from session to session.
- If you choose to include a learning activity, gather the materials you will need.
  - For Activity 1 you will need a strip of white cloth for each student, washable markers, a bowl of water and towels.
  - For Activity 2 you will need a framed picture for which the glass in front of the picture is grimy, soiled, and smudged. You will also need glass cleaner and paper towels.

Teaching Points

- God created everything good, beautiful, and noble.
- God wants your thoughts and actions to be pure.
- The good, beautiful, and noble things that enter our lives will be reflected in our relationship with God and others.

Say

It's hard to keep things clean in this world. We may scrub the toilet or disinfect the kitchen sink five times a day, but it won't keep tiny germs from growing. Even the food we eat contains tiny pieces of dirt and bug parts that are so small that they are almost impossible to remove. We just go ahead and eat them because we don't see them or taste them. Purity in food and in our life can be a hard thing to achieve.

However, God is perfectly pure and holy. Everything He created is good, beautiful, and noble. And because we are created in His image, He wants us to reflect His goodness, purity, and beauty as well.

This doesn't mean that we can't get mud on our shoes or that we have to brush our teeth three times a day (although that's a good thing to do). It means that our actions and our thoughts should be pure and holy. It's important that what we read, watch, and listen to is good because that is what reflects in our relationship with God and others.

Good thoughts and actions glorify God because they're a part of what it means to worship Him. Purity in our thoughts and in our actions demonstrates to God that we want to follow Him and actually be like Him. God wants your thoughts and actions to be pure.

Activity Options

Activity 1:*Pure Life.* Give each student a white strip of white cloth and a washable marker. Have them share things in their lives that are not pure, right, lovely and excellent (i.e. cheating, lying, talking back, making fun). Tell them to write one of those things on the cloth with the marker. Have students dip their cloth in the bowl of water and bring out-clean and pure. Share that our life is like the cloth which God can make clean. God wants our thoughts and actions to be pure.

Activity 2: *Clean or dirty.* Show the students a framed picture for which the glass in front of the picture is grimy, soiled, and smudged. As you clean the glass, note how it makes the picture so much easier to see. When we think impure, mean, or ugly thoughts we smudge and distort our relationship with God. It's harder to tell what His love for us looks like because all this dirt and grime is in the way. Pure thoughts and actions keep our understanding of God and His will for our lives from being clouded.

Action Point
Think about what you've thought about and how you've acted over the past week. Ask God to help you keep your thoughts and actions pure and good.

Prayer

Lord, help us to surround ourselves with things that are good, beautiful, noble, and lovely so we might glorify You. Amen.

For Next Time

God has given us each good and beautiful talents and abilities that can help express His love and truth to others. Next week we'll talk about how we can better use what He has given to each one of us.

Self

19 I can use my talents and abilities to please God.

Before You Begin

- Read 1 Corinthians 10:31, 1 Corinthians 12:27–31, and 1 Peter 4:11.
- Review the Teaching Points to familiarize yourself with the ideas to emphasize in this session.
- Read the session plan and select the elements that you will include.
- Choose a Bible memorization technique from those listed on page 122. Be sure to vary your teaching technique from session to session.
- If you choose to include a learning activity, gather the materials you will need.
  - For Activity 1 you will need paper and pencils for each student.

Teaching Points

- God has given each of us many different talents and abilities.
- I can use my talents and abilities to please God.
- Everything we say or do should glorify and please God.

Say

Michael Jordan was the NBA's most valuable player five times. He led the league in scoring a record ten seasons. He scored in the double digits 842 games in a row. His team, the Chicago Bulls, won six championships while he was playing with them. There are a lot of people who look up to and want to be like Michael Jordan because he was one of the greatest basketball players ever. There are not many people who play basketball as well as he did. But most of us can name something that we are very good at and that we enjoy doing.

Part of our special responsibility as humans who are in a relationship with God is to offer ourselves to Him in worship through our talents and abilities. But we are all unique—so all of us have different talents and abilities that help us glorify God. Some of you may be better at something than anyone else you know. Some of you may be talented at several things. However, we should honor and glorify God not just in the special things we do well, like our specific talents, but we should glorify Him in everything we do. Even common abilities, such as listening to people or helping someone mow their lawn, can help to demonstrate our love for God. Using our talents and abilities for God is like thanking Him for creating and loving us. You can use your talents and abilities to please God.

Activity Options

Activity 1: *Pass it on.* Have each student write his or her name on the top of a piece of paper, then pass their paper to the person to their right. That student writes something that they appreciate about the student whose name is on the top of the paper. Continue passing papers around until each student has his or her own paper back.

Activity 2: *Talent show.* Share your talents and abilities with others. Create a program that your class can present at a local nursing home or to the senior adult class in your church. Children can sing, tell a joke, play an instrument, draw a picture, juggle, etc.

Action Point

You can probably name at least one thing that you do really well. How can you use that talent or ability this week to show your love for God and others?

Prayer

Lord, thank You for giving each one of us talents and abilities to enjoy and use. Help us to always use these gifts to glorify You. Amen.

For Next Time

Our talents and abilities help express how much we appreciate our relationship with God. Next week we'll talk about a very special person who helps us with that relationship.

Jesus

Memory Verse

The Son is the radiance of God's glory and the exact representation of his being, sustaining all things by his powerful word. Hebrews 1:3

20 Jesus is the Son of God.

Before You Begin

- Read Matthew 16:13–20 and John 1.
- Review the Teaching Points to familiarize yourself with the ideas to emphasize in this session.
- Read the session plan and select the elements that you will include.
- Choose a Bible memorization technique from those listed on page 122. Be sure to vary your teaching technique from session to session.
- If you choose to include a learning activity, gather the materials you will need.
  - For Activity 2 you will need Bibles and the worksheet found on page 135.

Teaching Points

- Jesus is the Son of God.
- God sent His son, Jesus, to earth.
- We know God because we have Jesus.

Say

A lot of people from different religions around the world will talk about gods. They may believe in one god like we do. They may say their god is even powerful and strong like ours. But because we are Christians, we have some very exceptional, even astonishing, beliefs about our God. We believe that our God came to earth as a human, in the form of Jesus Christ.

Some people believe that Jesus, the son of Mary and Joseph of Nazareth, was just a great prophet and teacher. But Christians believe that Jesus was a very special man. We believe everything that is true of God is true of Jesus as well.

Hebrews 1:2 tells us that God created the universe through His Son. Jesus is God the Son. Because Jesus *is* God, He has all the authority of

God. John 13:3 says, "Jesus knew that the Father had put all things under his power, and that he had come from God and was returning to God." And unlike any other human before Him, He lived a sinless life. He did this because He was also God.

It's important for us to know exactly who Jesus is if we want to know God because He is God. Luke 10:22 says, "No one knows who the Son is except the Father, and no one knows who the Father is except the Son and those to whom the Son chooses to reveal him." God the Father chooses to reveal himself through God the Son, Jesus. He is the ultimate image and expression of God's love here on earth. He alone is perfectly able to understand and carry out the will of God.

Jesus is the Son of God.

Activity Options

Activity 1: *Image of God.* God created each of us in His image, and we all have characteristics and traits that are like His. But Jesus *is* God, an exact representation. Ask the students to name some of the characteristics and attributes of God (loving, caring, holy, etc.). Discuss how Jesus, a human, was exactly like God. Then ask the students how that might encourage them to know that Jesus lived a perfect life and was exactly like God even though He was also a human.

Activity 2: *Unscramble.* Have the students unscramble the words on the worksheet found on page 135. Discuss the meaning of each of the words in relation to Jesus' character.

Action Point

Because Jesus, who was God, came to earth as a human, we can understand God and His character better. Remember to thank God this week for sending Jesus to help us understand His character better.

Prayer

Lord, we thank You for Your Son, who has shown us what You are like. Thank You for showing us Your wisdom, power, and love in Jesus Christ. Amen.

For Next Time

This week we talked about Jesus being just like God. Next week we'll talk about how Jesus lived on earth not only as God but also as a man.

Jesus

21 Jesus lived on earth.

Before You Begin

■ Read John 1 Hebrews 1:3.
■ Review the Teaching Points to familiarize yourself with the ideas to emphasize in this session.
■ Read the session plan and select the elements that you will include.
■ Choose a Bible memorization technique from those listed on page 122. Be sure to vary your teaching technique from session to session.
■ If you choose to include a learning activity, gather the materials you will need.
  ● For Activity 1 you will need a small animal, such as a fish or an insect.

Teaching Points

■ Jesus came to earth as a human.
■ Jesus lived on earth.
■ As a human, Jesus experienced life as we experience it.

Say

God entered history as a human. We call it "the Incarnation," which literally means "en-flesh-ment." God had skin, bones, fingernails, a big toe, and even a belly button! That's a very amazing thing, but actually, Jesus' life was very ordinary. He was born to a woman named Mary in a little town called Bethlehem. He came to earth as a baby, so he cried, spit up, and cooed just like babies do. He grew up in another small town called Nazareth in a typical Jewish family. His father, Joseph, trained him to be a carpenter. It wasn't until He was thirty years old that He began His ministry of preaching, teaching, and healing people.

Sometimes, however, it's the seemingly insignificant things that make such a big difference. Because He lived such an ordinary life here on earth, He knows what it's like to be a human, just like you and me. He knows how much it hurts to stub your toe. He also knows what it's like to feel left out. Jesus couldn't have identified with some of our everyday happiness and frustrations if He had not lived a life like ours. We can see through His ordinary life that it's possible to be what God intended for us to be—good, honest, kind, and loving. All this is because Jesus lived on earth.

Activity Options

Activity 1: *Getting to know you.* Bring a small animal, such as a fish or a bug, to class. Ask the children, if they wanted to communicate with this animal, what they would need to do. The best thing they could do to understand the animal is to become the animal by taking on its appearance, habits, and form of communication. Discuss how Jesus understands us because He became like us.

Activity 2: *Incarnation.* Have the students list ways in which they think Jesus was just like them. Emphasize that He grew up, just like them, played games, slept, ate, drank, etc. Ask them how this helps them to more easily relate to God.

Action Point

We can have confidence that Jesus understands what it's like to be a human because He became a human.

Prayer

Lord, we thank You for Your Son, who lived, walked, and talked with us to show us exactly what Your love means for us. Amen.

For Next Time

Isn't it amazing that Jesus could be both God and man? Next week we'll talk more about what that means and what it says about the God we serve.

Jesus

22 Jesus is both God and human.

Before You Begin

- Read Philippians 2:6–7, 1 Timothy 3:16, and Hebrews 1.
- Review the Teaching Points to familiarize yourself with the ideas to emphasize in this session.
- Read the session plan and select the elements that you will include.
- Choose a Bible memorization technique from those listed on page 122. Be sure to vary your teaching technique from session to session.
- If you choose to include a learning activity, gather the materials you will need.
  - For Activity 1 you will need copies of the worksheet found on page 136 for each student.

Teaching Points

- Jesus is completely God and completely human.
- When Jesus came to earth, He did not lose His divinity but took on humanity.
- Jesus was called "Emmanuel," which means "God with us."

Say

Imagine what it would be like to lose the ability to communicate. You wouldn't be able to use the Internet or a cell phone, and what's worse, you wouldn't be able to talk or use facial expressions. Some people who cannot hear are still able to communicate very well with their hands and gestures. Some people who cannot speak can write or draw pictures. Our bodies truly are wonderful communicators. They not only help us to tell others what we're thinking and feeling, but they also tell us when we are getting sick or when our stomachs are full. In fact, it's nearly impossible to express a thought or idea without using our body or the things around us.

We know that God communicates with us in many ways. We can talk to God through prayer, and we can hear Him speak through Scripture. But

God has used more than just words to communicate His love to us. He's used the whole body. When Jesus came to earth, He became human. This is what we mean when we talk about the Incarnation or the "en-flesh-ment" of Jesus Christ. However, Jesus did not stop being God when He came to earth. He was fully God and fully human at the same time. Sometimes we call Jesus "Emmanuel" because it sums up what He was trying to communicate—He is "God with us." Amazingly, Jesus was able to perfectly embody love and provide a perfect example of what all humans should be like. Jesus is both God and human.

Activity Options

Activity 1: *God and man*. Using the worksheet found on page 136, have the students decide whether the actions show Jesus' humanity or His divinity.

Activity 2: *Incarnation*. Have the students create a special poem or an acrostic using the word I-N-C-A-R-N-A-T-I-O-N. Use words or phrases that describe Jesus as God or Jesus as man.

Action Point

God sent Jesus as a man to show His love for us. God can also work through you to show others that He loves them. How can you show the love of God to others this week?

Prayer

Lord, thank You for being a God who is always with us. You are always communicating Your love for us. Help us to celebrate Your presence in the world today. Amen.

For Next Time

As God and man, Jesus was able to do things for us that we cannot do for ourselves. Next week we will be learning more about the special person Jesus is and what He has done for us.

Jesus

Memory Verse

For we do not have a high priest who is unable to sympathize with our weaknesses, but we have one who has been tempted in every way, just as we are—yet was without sin. Hebrews 4:15

23 Jesus was tempted but did not sin.

Before You Begin

- Read Luke 4:1–13, Hebrews 2:18, and Hebrews 4:14–16.
- Review the Teaching Points to familiarize yourself with the ideas to emphasize in this session.
- Read the session plan and select the elements that you will include.
- Choose a Bible memorization technique from those listed on page 122. Be sure to vary your teaching technique from session to session.
- If you choose to include a learning activity, gather the materials you will need.
  - For Activity 1 you will need old magazines, scissors, poster board, and glue.
  - For Activity 2 you will need a few stones, a small stepstool, and several glasses of water.

Teaching Points

- As a human, Jesus had desires like us.
- Jesus was tempted but did not sin.
- Though we are tempted, we can choose not to sin.

Say

A couple of weeks ago, we talked about how Jesus, who is God, came to earth as a man. Because he was human like us, He had a belly button and a nose, had to go to bed, and often needed a bath, just like we do. Jesus had desires like we do. He got hungry, thirsty, frustrated, and tired, just like us. And just as we often are, Jesus was also tempted to fulfill selfish desires rather than follow God's will. The Bible tells us that Jesus was actually tempted three times. Jesus was in the wilderness praying and talking with the Father. He was very hungry. The devil came and suggested He turn stones into bread. Jesus said, "No." The second time Satan came, he argued that if Jesus was who He said He was, angels should come and take care of Him. Jesus said, "No." The third time the devil came he took Jesus to a high point where they could look over Jerusalem. The devil offered Jesus the world. But Jesus replied, "No." Finally the devil left.

These are things we all may be tempted by—things that are good, but if done for selfish reasons can separate us from God. They may be beautiful to look at, they may fill a hunger we crave, and they may even give us everything we've ever dreamed of. Jesus knew these things were tempting, but He said no. And because of Him, we can too. Jesus was tempted but did not sin.

Activity Options

Activity 1: *Temptation*. Have students look through old magazines and cut out pictures of tempting things, such as luxury cars, jewelry, etc. Glue these to the poster board on which you've written today's verse.

Activity 2: *Three Temptations*. Read the story of Jesus' temptation (Matthew 4:1–11) aloud to the class. As you read it, the students act out the story. One can be Jesus, one can be the tempter, and the rest can be angels. Allow them to use props, such as stones, a small stepstool, and glasses of water.

Action Point

What kinds of things often tempt you? Ask Jesus to help you to resist, just like He did. **Prayer**

Lord, although You were tempted, we rejoice that You did not give in to sin. We thank You for Your example, and we are glad You can help us to resist temptation. Amen.

For Next Time

You might think that only secret agents and spies get special missions, but Jesus had the most important mission of anyone who has ever lived. Next week we'll learn about this mission and what it has to do with us.

Jesus

24 Jesus came to be our Savior.

Before You Begin

- Read Luke 2:11, Luke 19:10, John 3:17, Galatians 4:4–7, and 1 John 4:14.
- Review the Teaching Points to familiarize yourself with the ideas to emphasize in this session.
- Read the session plan and select the elements that you will include.
- Choose a Bible memorization technique from those listed on page 122. Be sure to vary your teaching technique from session to session.
- If you choose to include a learning activity, gather the materials you will need.
  - For Activity 1 you will need to gather several objects that distinguish different vocations, such as letters and a mailbag for a mail carrier, or a hammer and a screwdriver for a carpenter.
  - For Activity 2 you will need to gather several symbols of a prophet (a scroll, a Bible), a priest (praying hands, an offering plate), and a king (a scepter, a crown).

Teaching Points

- The Son, Jesus Christ, had a special purpose in coming to earth.
- Jesus came to be our savior.
- Jesus is our savior because of what He did.

Say

What do you call someone who works at the post office and delivers mail? A mail carrier. What do you call someone who builds things out of wood? A carpenter. We know a mail carrier is a mail carrier and a carpenter is a carpenter because of what they do. They have a specific title because they do a specific job that only people with their titles do.

We call Jesus our savior because He did some very special things that only a savior can do. It was not only because who He was—God and human—but because of what He did that we can call Him our savior. A title like savior tells us what Jesus has done—He saved us from sin and death.

Jesus worked at three jobs in order to help us understand His title of savior; He was a prophet, a priest, and a king. We might see Him working at His different jobs at different times and in different places. And just like the mail carrier, Jesus has been given special titles because of the jobs He has.

We call Jesus a prophet because He spent a lot of His time here on earth preaching, teaching, and healing. He is also a priest because He offered himself as a sacrifice on our behalf. Finally, He is a king because even now He empowers, guides, and protects us. These aren't jobs that we usually hear of or see in offices, but they are the jobs that Jesus did to be our savior. Jesus came to be our savior.

Activity Options

Activity 1: *Vocational symbols*. Show the students the different symbols that you have brought to class and ask them to guess who uses them. Emphasize that we all have roles, and Jesus' role in coming to earth was to be our savior.

Activity 2: *Jesus' vocation.* Just as you showed the students different symbols for various vocations in Activity 1, show them the objects that you have brought to symbolize Jesus' roles as a prophet, priest, and king. As you show each object, discuss the ways in which Jesus lived out these roles as He was on earth.

Action Point

Jesus fulfilled His mission of being our savior through the roles of a prophet, priest, and king. We can reflect those jobs in our ministry on earth today as well by telling someone about Jesus, praying for others, and helping someone in need.

Prayer

Lord, thank You for loving us so much that you came to be our savior. We celebrate the completion of Your mission here on earth through Your life, death, and resurrection. Amen.

For Next Time

Nobody likes pain or suffering, but that was a part of Jesus' mission as Savior. As we learn more about Jesus' mission on earth, we'll find out just how far He went to complete it.

Jesus

25 Jesus died on the cross.

Before You Begin

- Read Matthew 27:32–56 and Hebrews 12:2.
- Review the Teaching Points to familiarize yourself with the ideas to emphasize in this session.
- Read the session plan and select the elements that you will include.
- Choose a Bible memorization technique from those listed on page 122. Be sure to vary your teaching technique from session to session.
- If you choose to include a learning activity, gather the materials you will need.
  - For Activity 1 you will need a small cross.
  - For Activity 2 you will need materials for each student to make a cross from pieces of bark, glue, and red yarn.

Teaching Points

- Jesus' mission to be our savior included His own suffering and death.
- Jesus' suffering occurred throughout His life.
- Jesus ultimately suffered death on the cross.

Say

All of us hate to experience pain. Even if it's simply an allergy or flu shot, we don't look forward to the few seconds of pain we know we will have to feel. The heart of Jesus' mission as Savior was to save us and show us how much He loves us. To do that, Jesus knew he would endure a lot of pain throughout His life, and, eventually die on a cross for us.

Jesus experienced more than just the physical pain of being beaten and nailed to a cross. He was also hurt by the insults and abuse of the crowd who witnessed his anguish. He was betrayed by one of His closest friends. He was rejected by the very people He was trying to help. He carried the full weight of human anger, violence, and sin upon His shoulders as He hung on the cross. Jesus suffered to the point of dying as both God and as man, so He understands perfectly when we feel lonely, rejected, or hurt by others. These are things that we usually try to avoid. But He didn't.

Even though Jesus didn't deserve to die, He willingly did it because He had a special mission to complete. He went through all of this suffering and pain because He loves us that much. Jesus died on the cross.

Activity Options

Activity 1: *Symbol*. Pass a cross around to each of the students. Explain that the cross is the central symbol of the Christian faith because it reminds us of what Jesus did for us.

Activity 2: *The cross.* Have the students make a simple cross from two pieces of bark or wood to remember how Jesus died for us. Form the cross with the two pieces of wood and fix with glue. Secure by wrapping a piece of yarn around the center of the cross.

Action Point

Have you ever felt rejection from a friend? Think about how that felt and what it might mean for Jesus to experience that kind of suffering for you.

Prayer

Lord, we remember the pain and suffering that You experienced on our behalf. Help us to find our strength in You when we feel pain or rejection because You, more than anyone else, understand. Amen.

For Next Time

This week we learned about the pain and suffering that Jesus experienced on the cross. Next week we'll find out the rest of the story of Jesus' mission here on earth.

Jesus

Memory Verse
But Christ has indeed been raised
from the dead, the firstfruits of those
who have fallen asleep. 1 Corinthians 15:20

26 God raised Jesus from the dead.

Before You Begin

- Read John 20, Acts 2:24, and Romans 6:4.
- Review the Teaching Points to familiarize yourself with the ideas to emphasize in this session.
- Read the session plan and select the elements that you will include.
- Choose a Bible memorization technique from those listed on page 122. Be sure to vary your teaching technique from session to session.
- If you choose to include a learning activity, gather the materials you will need.
  - For Activity 1 you will need a coffee filter, a pipe cleaner, and a wooden clothes pin for each child, water color pallets, brushes, cups of water, a cookie sheet or drying rack, glue, a fan, and a magnetic strip (optional).
  - For Activity 2 you will need large blank newsprint or paper, pencils, and Bibles.

Teaching Points

- After Jesus was crucified, His body was laid in a tomb for three days.
- God raised Jesus from the dead.
- After Jesus was resurrected, the disciples met with Him for forty days and witnessed his ascension to heaven.

Say

When Jesus suffered and died on the cross, He experienced the worst parts of human life, like physical pain, loneliness, and rejection. He allowed himself to suffer in this way just for us. But Jesus' mission to be our savior didn't end with his death on the cross. He did something that no one else had ever done before so we would be saved.

After Jesus was crucified, his body was put in a tomb, where it remained for three days. Several women, including his mother, went to prepare his body for final burial. When they arrived at the tomb, they were shocked that somebody was already there. This person was sitting on the tomb, and he told them that Jesus was not in the tomb. Jesus was alive! The women went to go tell the other disciples. Jesus had been raised from the dead!

In the forty days following His resurrection, Jesus stayed with His disciples. Some people could not believe that He was anything more than a ghost. But one of His disciples, Thomas, touched His wounds. Jesus' friends actually ate and drank with Him.

We celebrate Jesus' resurrection at Easter, but every Sunday is actually a celebration of that important event. When Jesus rose from the dead, He proved that He had accomplished His mission of salvation. Sin and death were no longer inevitable. Jesus conquered sin and death by being resurrected from the dead.

Activity Options

Activity 1: *Butterfly*. The butterfly is a wonderful symbol for the resurrection. Have each child use water colors to paint a coffee filter. Place on a cookie sheet and allow time to dry. Hint: Paint the coffee filters before you begin the lesson and let the filters dry in front of a fan. By the end of the lesson they should be dry enough to continue. Gather the filter in center and secure with a pipe cleaner. Glue to wooden clothes pin. Clip ends of pipe cleaner and glue to clothes pin for antennae. These can be clipped or mounted with a magnet.

Activity 2: *Good news!* Create a newspaper together based on the Matthew/Luke accounts of the resurrection. Make sure the students answer the questions *Who? What? Where? When? Why?* and *How?* Have students (individually or in groups) write the headline story. Some can draw pictures showing the events of the resurrection.

Action Point

Because Jesus died and was resurrected, we can have victory over death and sin. How can you celebrate this today?

Prayer

Lord, today we celebrate Your resurrection, for it brings us freedom from sin and death. Help us to remember and celebrate Your resurrection each day as we grow in relationship with You.

For Next Time

We know now that Jesus came to earth to be our savior, but why do you think He needed to do that for us? Next week we'll find out.

Salvation

27 All people have done wrong.

Before You Begin

- Read Romans 5:12, Ephesians 2:1–5, and 1 John 1:8–10.
- Review the Teaching Points to familiarize yourself with the ideas to emphasize in this session.
- Read the session plan and select the elements that you will include.
- Choose a Bible memorization technique from those listed on page 122. Be sure to vary your teaching technique from session to session.
- If you choose to include a learning activity, gather the materials you will need.
  - For Activity 1 you will need balloons, small pieces of paper, a broom or whisk, a wastebasket, and a dustpan.

Teaching Points

- Adam and Eve were the first people to sin.
- Sin is not God's intention for us.
- All people have done wrong, or sinned.

Say

We can be thankful that Jesus accomplished His mission to save us through His life, death, and resurrection. But why did we need to be saved? What was He saving us from?

The fact is that none of us are as good as God wanted us to be when He created us. Because God is perfect, we can only have a relationship with Him if we are perfect too.

Way back when Adam and Even stood underneath the Tree of Knowledge of Good and Evil, eating the fruit they had just picked, they disobeyed God. They were deciding not to trust God and the relationship they had with Him. They thought they could be like God without being in relationship with Him. They thought they could do it on their own. They didn't think they needed anyone else telling them what to do. So they ate the fruit. They soon found out that something was terribly wrong. While God still loved them and tried to protect them, the beautiful relationship they had enjoyed with God in the garden had changed forever because of their decision.

Just like Adam and Eve, we all make bad decisions—decisions that are selfish, proud, greedy, and independent of God. All people have done wrong. We call this sin. Sin and the effect of sin, which is death, separates us from God. Rather than living, talking, and loving God, we have decided that we can do things on our own and that we don't need anyone telling us what we should and shouldn't do. Perhaps you are jealous of your friend or brother or sister, or maybe you have disobeyed your parents. When you did that, you committed a sin. All people have sinned.

Activity Options

Activity 1: *Confession clean-up.* In this relay, students must run down to a bag of blown-up balloons filled with sins (written on small pieces of paper), pop the balloon, and say the sin out loud. Then they must sweep the small paper with the sin to the trash can sitting at the starting line. Once they have picked up the sin with the dustpan and thrown it in the trash, the next person may go. After you've finished playing the game, remind the students that we have all sinned, but God is faithful to forgive those sins when we confess them to Him.

Action Point

We all make bad decisions that hurt God at some point in our lives. Can you remember something you've done that was wrong? You can tell God about it today.

Prayer

Lord, we are sorry for what we have done wrong by being selfish, proud, or disobedient. Please help us as we try to make good decisions as we follow You. Amen.

For Next Time

We've all sinned. So, if everyone's done it, what's the big deal? Next week we'll talk about why sin is so bad and what it does to our relationship with God.

Salvation

Memory Verse

No one who lives in him keeps on sinning. No one who continues to sin has either seen him or known him. 1 John 3:6

28 Sin separates people from God.

Before You Begin

- Read Psalm 51, Isaiah 59:2, and Ephesians 2:12–13.
- Review the Teaching Points to familiarize yourself with the ideas to emphasize in this session.
- Read the session plan and select the elements that you will include.
- Choose a Bible memorization technique from those listed on page 122. Be sure to vary your teaching technique from session to session.
- If you choose to include a learning activity, gather the materials you will need.
  - For Activity 1 you will need a glass of water, a cup of vegetable oil, and a spoon.

Teaching Points

- Sin is bad because it separates us from God.
- Sin makes us less than what God made us to be.
- God wants us to have a good relationship with Him because He knows it is best for us.

Say

Have any of your good friends ever moved away? Maybe they moved to another school, another city, or even another state. It's hard to remain good friends when you're far away from each other. You may still like each other, but since you're not around each other as much, you don't talk as often. You get too busy, and you make other friends. You have to work twice as hard when you're farther away from someone to keep that friendship going.

When we have sin in our lives, it separates us from God, and it hurts our relationship, just like distance between you and a good friend hurts your friendship. Eventually, because we're not close to God, we forget what He's like. We forget that He made us, protects us, and loves us. We are so concerned with ourselves that we forget that God created us to be like Him. We might even think we don't need God anymore, so we don't even admit that we have a relationship with God. In fact, we may do something completely opposite of what God would want us to do—we may lie, think we can do things on our own, and treat other people badly.

Because Jesus loved us so much, He gave us the freedom to choose to be in relationship with Him. He's never forced us, and yet sometimes we still don't trust Him enough to acknowledge or admit our need for Him. God wants what is best for us, which means avoiding sin and having a relationship with Him. And to grow in that relationship, we must continually seek Him and remember that sin separates us from Him.

Activity Options

Activity 1: *Oil and water.* This simple object lesson demonstrates how contradictory God and sin are to each another. As you pour water into a glass, say, "There are some things that are very similar to God. We are made in His image, and we are meant to be in relationship with Him. But sin is something that is not like God. In fact it's the exact opposite."

Then pour a cup of oil into the cup. Stir the oil and watch it separate from the water. Then say, "In fact, God and sin can never come together, and when we have sin in our lives, it keeps us separated from God as well."

Action Point

Have you ever felt separated from God because of sinful thoughts or actions? You can restore that relationship by asking forgiveness and keeping close to Him through Bible reading and prayer.

Prayer

Lord, we are sorry that we sometimes separate ourselves from You. Help us to sense that You are near and will never leave us. Amen.

For Next Time

Thank goodness we don't have to be separated from God! Next week we'll find out about something God does for us even though we don't deserve it.

Salvation

Memory Verse

But God demonstrates his own love for us in this: While we were still sinners, Christ died for us. Romans 5:8

29 God loves us even though we have sinned.

Before You Begin

- Read John 3:16, 1 Peter 3:18, 1 John 3:16, and 1 John 4:9–10.
- Review the Teaching Points to familiarize yourself with the ideas to emphasize in this session.
- Read the session plan and select the elements that you will include.
- Choose a Bible memorization technique from those listed on page 122. Be sure to vary your teaching technique from session to session.
- If you choose to include a learning activity, gather the materials you will need.
  - For Activity 1 you will need a wallet, an I.D., and a twenty-dollar bill.
  - For Activity 2 you will need clothespins with springs.

Teaching Points

- God wants to be in relationship with us because He created us.
- Our separation from God does not diminish His love for us.
- God loves us even though we have sinned.

Say

Have you ever done something for someone, such as cleaning a room or taking out their trash, even though they never asked you to do it? Perhaps it was for someone who had never done anything nice for you. What would cause you to do something like that? It's probably because you want to show someone how much you love him or her.

Though we have done nothing to deserve it, God lavishly demonstrates His great love for us by pursuing a relationship with us. Even though we have separated ourselves from God, He still wants to walk and talk with us. That's why He created us—not to just exist, but to reflect His image. We were meant to love God and to love others. That means He loved us enough to give us the freedom to choose to be in relationship with Him. And even when we choose to do wrong—to hurt God or others—He is still concerned about us. This is called grace. Even when we don't deserve His love and protection, He offers it to us anyway. God loves us even though we have sinned.

Jesus' mission to be our savior is so important because it proves that God loves us. It shows us just how much He still loves us even though we have separated ourselves from Him.

Activity Options

Activity 1: *Understanding grace.* Place an I.D. and a twenty-dollar bill in a wallet. Ask the children, "If you found this wallet on the street, what would you do with it? It has twenty dollars in it. Would you keep it? What if you decided to return it? To return it just as you found would be showing its owner mercy. It's giving what's expected or fair. But what if you gave this wallet back to its owner and put another twenty-dollar bill in it? Does the owner deserve another twenty dollars for losing the wallet? Giving over and above what is deserved or expected is showing someone grace."

Activity 2: *Grace give-away.* Designate an area in the classroom as the play area. Give each student five clothespins to hold in their hands. The object of the game is to get rid of all the clothespins in their hands by pinning them on someone else. The first person to have no more clothes pins wins the round. At the end of the game, say, "God doesn't just make grace available and then do nothing. He pursues us in His love to give us grace, just like you tried so hard to give away your clothespins."

Action Point

Today, we've talked about God's grace for us. We can reflect God's image by showing others grace.

Prayer

Lord, we thank you for loving us even though we have sinned and separated ourselves from you. Help us to show love for others, even when we might think they don't deserve it. Amen.

For Next Time

If you've ever made a promise, you know how important it is to keep it. God has made a promise to us that He is sure to keep. Next week we will find out what that promise is.

Salvation

30 God sent His Son to forgive sins.

Before You Begin

- Read Luke 24:46–47, Romans 3:22–25, Ephesians 1:7, and Colossians 1:13–14.
- Review the Teaching Points to familiarize yourself with the ideas to emphasize in this session.
- Read the session plan and select the elements that you will include.
- Choose a Bible memorization technique from those listed on page 122. Be sure to vary your teaching technique from session to session.
- If you choose to include a learning activity, gather the materials you will need.
  - For Activity 1 you will need a map of Florida that includes the Keys.
  - For Activity 2 you will need building blocks.

Teaching Points

- God showed the extent of His love by sending His son to earth.
- Through Jesus, God provided a way for us to enter into a relationship with Him.
- God sent His son to forgive our sins.

Say

Some of the longest bridges in the world cross miles of water just to connect two pieces of land. The Overseas Highway in Florida spans water and land to connect all the islands around the mainland. It's 126 miles long and can take hours just to cross it. The Seven Mile bridge that is a part of this highway, connects Key Vach and Sunshine Key and is one of the longest bridges in the world.

People have tried other ways of crossing water besides bridges, but not all of them actually work. Ferries, rafts, sandbars, sea turtles, rope, and even swimming are all ways to cross a river or a body of water. But these can be slow, difficult, and even dangerous. A bridge is more direct and usually safer.

While Jesus lived as a human here on earth, He did things differently than any other human that had lived before. After sin had entered the world through the disobedience of Adam and Eve, we were all separated from God. There needed to be something to bring us back together, like a bridge. By sending His own son to earth, God showed us the extent of His love. God sent His son to forgive our sins. Jesus' life, death, and resurrection demonstrate goodness, justice, love, and holiness in terms humans can understand. It also provided a new way for us to enter into relationship with Him. Jesus Christ himself was the way to bridge the separation to the Father.

Activity Options

Activity 1: *Bridges*. Display a map of Florida with the Keys showing the span of the bridge connecting the Keys to the mainland. Emphasize once again that Jesus is like a bridge to God.

Activity 2: *Bridge of forgiveness*. Place several books and Bibles on the table. Have students construct bridges with building blocks from a Bible to a regular book that is about one foot away. Give a prize for the most creative bridge. Tell the students that the bridge is like Jesus making a way for us (the regular book) to be connected to God (the Bible).

Action Point

Without Jesus, separation from God is impossible to bridge. Have you asked Jesus to span the gap between you and God?

Prayer

Lord, we thank You for sending Jesus to bridge the separation between us. Help us this week to forgive one another as we learn to become more like You. Amen.

For Next Time

Jesus' mission was to bridge the separation between us and God. Next week we'll learn why Jesus' death on the cross means so much to us.

Salvation

Memory Verse

He himself bore our sins in his body on the tree, so that we might die to sins and live for righteousness; by his wounds you have been healed. 1 Peter 2:24

31 Jesus died to forgive my sin.

Before You Begin

- Read Acts 13:38, Colossians 2:13–15, Hebrews 10:1–18, and 1 John 2:2.
- Review the Teaching Points to familiarize yourself with the ideas to emphasize in this session.
- Read the session plan and select the elements that you will include.
- Choose a Bible memorization technique from those listed on page 122. Be sure to vary your teaching technique from session to session.
- If you choose to include a learning activity, gather the materials you will need.
  - For Activity 2 you will need bags of balloons, tape, and a timer.

Teaching Points

- Because God loves us, He provided atonement for our sins.
- Jesus died to forgive our sins.
- Jesus is the bridge between us and God.

Say

Who else can forgive sins but Jesus? We may be able to forgive a brother, sister, or a friend for something wrong they've done to us, but can we forgive them for something they've done to someone else? Only the person who was wronged can do that. Only Jesus is able to actually forgive all of us for all of the sins we've committed.

Jesus' mission to save us meant that He would forgive all of our sins. This forgiveness happened throughout His whole life. While He was here on earth, He forgave men and women, the crippled and the blind, the tax collector and the soldier.

But upon the cross, Jesus did what no other human has been able to do on their own. Jesus Christ, as both God and human, was the only person who could carry the sins of everyone and get rid of them forever.

Only Jesus could build the bridge between us and God. Jesus died to forgive our sin. Atonement literally means "at-one-ment". It brings two opposite things together. Jesus' life, death, and resurrection were the bridge that brought "at-one-ment" to God and humans.

The death that Jesus experienced on the cross involved great cost and sacrifice. But His death was an amazing and matchless expression of love and forgiveness.

Activity Options

Activity 1: *Atonement*. Have students create an acrostic poem using the word A-T-O-N-E-M-E-N-T. Encourage the students to use phrases that will help them understand what Jesus' death on the cross did for them.

Activity 2: *Balloon bridge building*. Set two tables apart from one another. Divide students into two teams and place them at separate tables. Give each team bags of balloons and scotch tape. They must begin building a balloon bridge from their table that connects to other table's balloon bridge without collapsing. Give them a certain amount of time to accomplish the task. At the end of the activity, emphasize once again that Jesus' death on the cross provided a bridge to God.

Action Point

We've talked a lot about forgiveness today. Have you asked God to forgive you of things you've done wrong? You can ask Him today.

Prayer

Lord, we are amazed and grateful that You love us so much that You would send Your son to suffer and die for us. We celebrate that we can be in a relationship with You. Help us to grow even closer to You. Amen.

For Next Time

Everyone loves to receive gifts. Next week we'll talk about one of the greatest gifts ever given.

Salvation

 32 ## God forgives those who believe in Jesus.

Before You Begin

- Read Acts 13:38–39, Romans 10:9–11, and Ephesians 1:7.
- Review the Teaching Points to familiarize yourself with the ideas to emphasize in this session.
- Read the session plan and select the elements that you will include.
- Choose a Bible memorization technique from those listed on page 122. Be sure to vary your teaching technique from session to session.
- If you choose to include a learning activity, gather the materials you will need.
  - For Activity 1 you will need a gift box, wrapped as a gift.
  - For Activity 2 you will need a bar of soap and a plastic knife or spoon for each student.

Teaching Points

- Our relationship with God begins when we confess our sins.
- We should ask God for forgiveness, which He freely gives.
- God forgives those who believe in Jesus.

Say

God the Son, Jesus, was sent by the Father to live on earth. Eventually Jesus died on the cross to save us from our sins. The forgiveness that Jesus' life, death, and resurrection brought has been offered to everyone. But not everyone chooses to enjoy the joy and freedom forgiveness brings.

It's like a gift that you might get that's a complete surprise. You don't know where it came from or what is in it, but you know it's from a very special person who went to a lot of trouble to give it to you. You probably would choose to tear into it and see what's inside. But some people don't do that with this incredible gift of forgiveness. Some people save it until it's the last gift to be opened, and so they don't have any time to enjoy it. Some may open the gift, but don't want it once they see what's inside. Some people are too afraid of the gift and refuse to even open it.

There are those, however, who do open the gift and gladly accept it. They have done two things. They have admitted they are sinners. Because they know they don't really deserve forgiveness, they understand that it is a very special gift. Secondly, they say what they believe: that Jesus is the one who has saved them from their sins. Those who confess their sins and confess Jesus as their savior can happily receive the gift of forgiveness. God forgives those who believe in Jesus.

Activity Options

Activity 1: *The gift.* Wrap a gift box in the most beautiful paper and bow you can find. Use this gift during the lesson to show how people receive the gift of forgiveness.

Activity 2: *Clean confession.* Our confession of doing wrong is one way we come clean with God. Use plastic knives to carve crosses into soft bars of soap. Shavings can be collected and mixed with water to form liquid soap.

Action Point

Have you received the gift of forgiveness from God? You can do it today, and it's as simple as A-B-C. Admit you have sinned. Believe in Jesus Christ. Confess Him as your savior.

Prayer

Lord, we confess that though we have done wrong, You have forgiven us. We confess that You are Lord of our lives, and today we receive this gift of forgiveness. Amen.

For Next Time

Next week we're going to talk about one of the good things that happens after we've accepted God's gift of forgiveness: we become part of a huge new family!

Salvation

Memory Verse

In love he predestined us to be adopted as his sons through Jesus Christ, in accordance with his pleasure and will. Ephesians 1:5

 33 We are adopted into God's family by faith.

Before You Begin

- Read Romans 8:12–17, Galatians 3:26–29, and 1 Peter 2:9–10.
- Review the Teaching Points to familiarize yourself with the ideas to emphasize in this session.
- Read the session plan and select the elements that you will include.
- Choose a Bible memorization technique from those listed on page 122. Be sure to vary your teaching technique from session to session.
- If you choose to include a learning activity, gather the materials you will need.
  - For Activity 1 you will need paper and crayons or colored pencils for each student. You will also need a church directory (if available).
  - For Activity 2 copy and distribute to each student worksheet "What's in a Name" found on page 137.

Teaching Points

- We are adopted into God's family by faith.
- God is a father and a brother to us.
- When we accept Jesus as our savior, we can take His name by calling ourselves Christians.

Say

If you've ever been to a family reunion, you could probably find many different kinds of relationships present. Families are made up of all kinds of people—moms, dads, aunts, uncles, nieces, nephews, and cousins. It's easy to lose track of all the relatives one family can have.

We become a part of a different kind of family when we confess that we have done wrong and that we believe in Jesus. When we make this confession, our relationship with God changes. We can treat Him like a Father because He protects and cares for us. And because of Jesus, He is also our brother; we can confide in Him and talk with Him. As a brother, Jesus is always looking out for us.

When we confess Jesus as our Lord, we not only gain God as Father and Jesus as Brother, but we also gain an entire family. This family is made up of all different kinds of people—big and small, black and white, young and old. And they are all brothers and sisters in Christ. We recognize our brothers and sisters because we have all taken the same name that identifies us as followers of Jesus: Christian.

Activity Options

Activity 1: *Family pictures.* Have each student draw a picture of his or her family. They can show the class who is in their family and name the different relationships. If your church has a directory with pictures, show it to the class and point out that all of the people in it are a part of the family of God.

Activity 2: *What's in a Name?* Work together in small groups or as a class and match the name with the correct definition of the name on the worksheet. You will find the answers to the worksheet on page 137.

Action Point

As we become a part of God's family, we take on the name of our big brother, Jesus. That's why people who look and act like Jesus are called Christians. How do people around you know you're part of this new family?

Prayer

Lord, thank You for inviting and welcoming us into Your family. We celebrate with our brothers and sisters the gift of life and forgiveness we have received. Amen.

For Next Time

Another part of God's amazing gift of forgiveness is eternal life. We will talk next week about how we can live forever because we know and love Jesus.

Salvation

Memory Verse
For my Father's will is that everyone who looks to the Son and believes in him shall have eternal life, and I will raise him up at the last day. John 6:40

34 We can live forever in heaven.

Before You Begin

- Read John 3:36, John 4:13–14, 2 Corinthians 5:1, and 1 John 2:25.
- Review the Teaching Points to familiarize yourself with the ideas to emphasize in this session.
- Read the session plan and select the elements that you will include.
- Choose a Bible memorization technique from those listed on page 122. Be sure to vary your teaching technique from session to session.
- If you choose to include a learning activity, gather the materials you will need.
  - For Activity 1 prepare copies of John 4:1-42 or Bible for each student, a white (light) scarf, a black (dark) scarf, large bucket and a cup.
  - For Activity 2 copy "Proof of Life Worksheet" found on page 138 and distribute to each student.

Teaching Points

- Because we believe in Jesus Christ, we also have the promise of eternal life.
- We can live forever in heaven.
- Jesus is life.

Say

Some things seem to live forever. The giant Redwood Sequoias in California will live for two to three thousand years. That means that a tree that old today would have been planted in 1000 B.C! Some of them are over 300 feet tall. There's one giant named General Sherman that is actually the largest tree in the world. It's 275 feet tall and 103 feet around. Eventually, however, even this tree will not grow any taller. Its needles will drop; its limbs will break. Even this giant redwood will die.

These trees are amazing because they live so long. Most people would say that they wish they too could live this long. Because we value our lives, we try to hold on to them and protect them. That's one reason we have hospitals and doctors. But Jesus told His followers that He was life. Because He was God, He had created life and He would protect life, even if He had to die to do it. We know He did die to save our lives. But Jesus was raised from the dead so that life could continue. He conquered death. In fact, Jesus promises eternal life to anyone who believes in Him. We believe that He lived, died, and rose again. We believe that someday we will follow Him in the resurrection. Our bodies won't last forever, but as we live like Him each day, we can experience new life in Him. But someday, we will receive new bodies as we live forever in heaven with Jesus.

Activity Options

Activity 1: *Bread of Life Skit.* As a class act out John 4:1-42. Have someone serve as a narrator, portray Jesus (white scarf), the Samaritan Woman (black scarf), the disciples and the village people.

Activity 2: *Proof of Life Worksheet.* Copy page 138 for distribution. Work individually, small groups or as a class to discover from scripture which statements are True and which are False.

Action Point

Thank Jesus for the opportunity He has given to us to live in heaven for eternity.

Prayer

Lord, today we celebrate our new life in You. Your life, death, and resurrection have brought us this wonderful gift. We look forward to following You each day and forever. Amen.

For Next Time

There's a lot to do before we spend eternity with Jesus. Next week we'll talk about who will help to carry out the mission Jesus has given us to accomplish here on earth.

Church

Memory Verse

And they sang a new song: "You are worthy to take the scroll and to open its seals, because you were slain, and with your blood you purchased men for God from every tribe and language and people and nation. You have made them to be a kingdom and priests to serve our God, and they will reign on the earth." Revelation 5:9–10

35 The Church is all believers everywhere.

Before You Begin

- Read Romans 12:4–8 and Ephesians 4:3–6.
- Review the Teaching Points to familiarize yourself with the ideas to emphasize in this session.
- Read the session plan and select the elements that you will include.
- Choose a Bible memorization technique from those listed on page 122. Be sure to vary your teaching technique from session to session.
- If you choose to include a learning activity, gather the materials you will need.
  - For Activity 1 you will need missions magazines or pictures of Christians who live in other countries.
  - For Activity 2 you will need a piece of paper, tape, and scissors for each student.

Teaching Points

- God's family gathers together to form the Church.
- The Church is all believers everywhere.
- Jesus gave the Church a mission to carry out.

Say

Wherever God's family meets together to worship Him, we call it the Church. The Church is not a building, an institution, or an organization. It's a group of people who believe in Jesus. People in the Church may even speak different languages or live in different countries, yet they all believe the same things. And these things are what make them God's children and a part of God's family.

What unites these people is that they all believe in God the Father, Son, and Holy Spirit. They also believe that Jesus, the Son, came to earth as a human. He lived, died, and rose from the dead to bring us salvation and forgive us of our sins. They have confessed their sins and received the gift of forgiveness. Finally, they believe that they are living out Jesus' mission today in the world.

Jesus told His disciples to go to all the world and tell others about Him. So even today believers everywhere live their lives so that Christ can be seen in them. Like a mirror, the Church everywhere reflects what Christ did for the world. And what did He do? He prayed to the Father, loved people, read Scripture, taught His disciples, and preached the good news. The Church around the world now does the same things. The Church is all believers everywhere.

Activity Options

Activity 1: *The Church.* Use missions magazines or videos from your denominational missions department to show that the Church includes all people who believe in Jesus, even if they speak different languages and live in different countries.

Activity 2: *Möbius strip.* Have the students put a piece of tape on one end of a strip of paper. Turn into a loop, but before attaching, flip one end of the paper over. This loop will have a half-twist in it. Cut down the middle of the strip. Instead of getting two separate strips, the Möbius strip becomes one long strip. (To start the cut off, fold the strip and make a small cut, then unfold the strip and use the hole as a starting point.) This loop of paper, even when cut, still links together to form one chain. This can provide a good illustration of how the Church may seem very diverse but is still linked by a common faith.

Action Point

Take time today to pray for your Christian brothers and sisters who are carrying out the mission Jesus has given us in different parts of the world.

Prayer

Lord, we thank You today for the Church, where we can come together with our brothers and sisters in Christ to worship and serve You. Help us to work together to fulfill the mission you gave us. Amen.

For Next Time

Our own church, right here in this town, is also a part of the body of Christ, and we have the same mission as everyone else who is a part of God's family. Next week we will discover what part we get to play in this exciting assignment.

Church

Memory Verse

For where two or three come together in my name, there am I with them.
Matthew 18:20

36 We belong to a local church.

Before You Begin

- Read Acts 2:42–47 and Hebrews 10:25.
- Review the Teaching Points to familiarize yourself with the ideas to emphasize in this session.
- Read the session plan and select the elements that you will include.
- Choose a Bible memorization technique from those listed on page 122. Be sure to vary your teaching technique from session to session.
- If you choose to include a learning activity, gather the materials you will need.
  - For Activity 1 you will need copies of the worksheet found on page 139 for each student.
  - For Activity 2 you will need a marble and a variety of cardboard tubes (those used for paper towels, wrapping paper, and toilet paper).

Teaching Points

- We belong to a local church.
- The mission of the Church is fulfilled through the local church.
- Local churches gather to pray, celebrate the sacraments, and serve.

Say

It's exciting to consider that we're a part of a Church that is worldwide. There are people who believe in Jesus like we do who live thousands of miles away. But because of the long distances, many languages, and different cultures, it would be impossible for all of us to gather together every Sunday. We may not see the whole Church in one place at one time, but we can still see the Church in action all the time.

Every week when you go to your local church, you see a smaller version of the worldwide Church living and worshipping together. The word "church" actually means "to gather." So wherever there are believers gathered to worship God, proclaim the good news, and serve in Jesus' name, the Church is present. In fact, our local church is just one of the places where the mission of the entire Church is carried out daily.

Scripture talks about how important local churches were in sharing the good news to everyone who would listen. Paul went on three missionary journeys to start and revisit local churches around Asia. These churches spent their time just like Jesus had taught His disciples to do—praying to the Father, reading Scripture, teaching disciples, and preaching the good news. Today local churches do the same thing. They serve their local communities by hosting weekly worship services, offering Communion, evangelizing, helping with missions around the world, and helping people in need.

We belong to a local church.

Activity Options

Activity 1: *Missionary maze.* Use the worksheet found on page 139 to show all the local churches Paul started on his missionary journeys. Using a Bible map trace the route Paul took.

Activity 2: *Marble madness.* Students learn to work together in this exercise. Give each student a cardboard tube of any size. Form two teams, and have each team stand in a line. They must pass a marble from one end of the line to the other using only their tubes. The team to get its marble to the end of the line the quickest wins. Stress that churches must work in harmony to fulfill their mission.

Action Point

What can you do in your local church to help support it?

Prayer

Lord, we thank You for our brothers and sisters in Christ who worship and serve together in this local church. Help us be Your witnesses in the community around us. Amen.

For Next Time

Becoming a part of God's family, or the Church, is a big event in our lives. We begin our new life with a very special celebration. We'll talk about this event next week.

Church

37 Baptism represents our new life in Christ.

Before You Begin

- Read Romans 6:3–5, Galatians 3:26–27, Colossians 2:11–12, and Hebrews 10:22.
- Review the Teaching Points to familiarize yourself with the ideas to emphasize in this session.
- Read the session plan and select the elements that you will include.
- Choose a Bible memorization technique from those listed on page 122. Be sure to vary your teaching technique from session to session.
- If you choose to include a learning activity, gather the materials you will need.
  - For Activity 1 you will need to ask your pastor to show the class your local church baptistery.
  - For Activity 2 you will need butterfly stickers or temporary tattoos for each student.

Teaching Points

- Baptism is our initiation into God's family.
- In baptism, we symbolically experience the life, death, and resurrection of Christ.
- A sacrament is an outward symbol of what is happening inside.
- Baptism represents our new life in Christ.

Say

You've probably all attended a wedding. The reason that people have public ceremonies is to officially declare to everyone and God that they are entering into marriage. When we become Christians, there is also a public ceremony in which we make an official announcement to let everyone know that we are joining the family of God. We call this event "baptism." There are a lot of changes going on, and there are important outward symbols that make the occasion memorable. We call these sacraments.

If you've seen someone be baptized, you know it can happen in different ways such as sprinkling, pouring, and going under the water. The important thing is that they get wet. Water is an important part of baptism because we do so many things with water. We clean with it. We drink it. We grow things with it. We really couldn't live without water. So when people go under the water, they are celebrating their new life in Jesus. They get to follow Jesus' life, death, and resurrection.

When Jesus gave His disciples the Church's mission, He gave them some simple instructions. The disciples needed to live their faith daily by reading Scripture, telling everybody about the good news of Jesus Christ, sharing in Communion, and baptizing in His name. That's what children in God's family do to live like Jesus. Baptism represents our new life in Christ.

Activity Options

Activity 1: *Baptistery tour.* Ask your pastor to give your class a tour of your local church baptistery. For children who have never been baptized, explain the process of baptism, what the pastor says, and the symbols that go along with the service.

Activity 2: *New life.* Baptism is a symbol and a seal of our new relationship with God. Butterflies can also symbolize our new life in Christ. Give each student a temporary tattoo or sticker that they can wear as a symbol of new life.

Action Point

Have you been baptized yet? If you believe that Jesus is Lord, consider discussing it with your parents or pastor.

Prayer

Lord, today we celebrate our new life in You. We enjoy being a part of Your family. As children of God, help us to become more like You each day. Amen.

For Next Time

Baptism is one sacrament. Next week we'll talk about another sacrament called the Lord's Supper.

Church

Memory Verse

For whenever you eat this bread and drink this cup, you proclaim the Lord's death until he comes.

1 Corinthians 11:26

38 The Lord's Supper represents Christ's sacrifice.

Before You Begin

- Read Luke 22:19–20, John 6:51–58, and 1 Corinthians 10:16–17.
- Review the Teaching Points to familiarize yourself with the ideas to emphasize in this session.
- Read the session plan and select the elements that you will include.
- Choose a Bible memorization technique from those listed on page 122. Be sure to vary your teaching technique from session to session.
- If you choose to include a learning activity, gather the materials you will need.
  - For Activity 1 you will need freshly baked bread and a bottle of grape juice.
  - For Activity 2 you will need a reproduction of Leonardo DaVinci's painting *The Last Supper*.

Teaching Points

- We celebrate the Lord's Supper to remember Christ's death on the cross.
- We celebrate the Lord's Supper to thank God for His grace and love for us shown in Jesus Christ.
- The Lord's Supper represents Christ's sacrifice.

Say

Don't you love the smell and taste of freshly baked bread or chocolate chip cookies? And who doesn't enjoy cuddling up by a fire with a warm, fuzzy blanket? In order to enjoy these things, we use our senses of taste, smell, and touch. Without our senses, much of life would be boring. We wouldn't be able to taste or smell good food or feel things that are soft.

Jesus used things that we taste, smell, and touch to teach us about who He is and what He has done for us. In fact, Jesus actually used a special meal to help His disciples understand this. Jesus used bread and wine to show them what He and His mission were like. Later on, that feast would help them remember how Jesus had lived and died for them. Eating this feast meant that they would willingly give their own lives to share the good news of Jesus with the world. And this feast helped them look forward to Jesus' return.

For the same reasons as Jesus' disciples, we also partake of bread and wine (or grape juice). We call it the Lord's Supper, because Jesus gave the first feast. After He left, His disciples in the Church broke bread and drank wine. We do the same thing because we know Jesus is near to us, and we can sense His presence as we remember Him, thank Him, and look forward to His return. The Lord's Supper represents Christ's sacrifice.

Activity Options

Activity 1: *Bread and wine.* Share freshly baked bread in the classroom so the room is filled with its aroma. Also have cold glasses of grape juice for each student. Not every loaf of bread or glass of grape juice is a Communion meal, but we set aside certain times when these foods do mean something more. It's important that we smell the bread and break it for one another. It's important that we taste the juice because it connects what we do everyday with what Jesus did for us in His life, death, and resurrection. (Be aware of possible allergies to the bread or grape juice.)

Activity 2: *Masterpiece.* Use Leonardo DaVinci's well-known masterpiece *The Last Supper* to help students visualize the original feast. (You can find copies of this painting on the Internet.

Action Point

Have you ever taken Communion? As you do, remember the special meaning of the Lord's Supper.

Prayer

Lord, we thank You for these special ways we have of remembering, celebrating, and thanking You for Your love for us. Amen.

For Next Time

One of the best things about being a part of God's family is that we get to help each other. We will talk about our responsibilities as brothers and sisters in Christ next week.

Church

Memory Verse
Each one should use whatever gift
he has received to serve others,
faithfully administering God's grace
in its various forms. 1 Peter 4:10

39 We serve others by helping at church.

Before You Begin

- Read Romans 12:3–13, 1 Corinthians 14:12–17, and Ephesians 6:7.
- Review the Teaching Points to familiarize yourself with the ideas to emphasize in this session.
- Read the session plan and select the elements that you will include.
- Choose a Bible memorization technique from those listed on page 122. Be sure to vary your teaching technique from session to session.
- If you choose to include a learning activity, gather the materials you will need.
  - For Activity 1 you will need masking tape.
  - For Activity 2 you will need paper and crayons or markers for each student.

Teaching Points

- We serve others by helping at church.
- The local church allows us to serve the world.
- We learn to love others by loving other brothers and sisters in Christ.

Say

What happens when every single organ, tissue, or part of your body isn't working together? You probably become sick. You can't go to school. You eat a lot of chicken soup. You can't play with friends until you're better.

Even if tiny body parts like your cells aren't working together, it can mean bad things for your body. A healthy body has all its parts working for and with each other.

Another name for the Church is the body of Christ. And just like our physical bodies, every part of the church needs to work together for it function properly. Jesus is the head of the Church and tells us what to do. But the Church cannot go into the world to share His good news if it doesn't work together. We may fight with one another, take on too much work, or even work against each other.

But God has given us talents and abilities so that they can be used to help the Church fulfill its mission in the world. We begin by serving our brothers and sisters in Christ. We help them to do their part of the mission Jesus has given us, and they help us do ours. It may seem like some parts of the body of Christ get more attention, but all the body parts need to serve for and with each other so that Jesus' mission can be carried out. We serve others by helping at church.

Activity Options

Activity 1: *Working together.* Divide the class into teams of two. As they stand together tape their inside wrists together with masking tape. Ask teams to complete tasks such as tying their shoes, opening cans of soft drinks, dumping out a box of crayons and putting them back. Stress the importance of all parts working together.

Activity 2: *Body parts.* Draw a large outline of a body on a large sheet of paper. Have the class label "parts" in the body of Christ based on 1 Corinthians 12:12–31. For example, they could label feet as missionaries, mouths as preachers, and hands as those who help with relief efforts.

Action Point

As children of God, we have offered our whole lives to God. But what do you offer to God that helps others?

Prayer

Lord, as Your body in the world, help us to love each other and work together to accomplish Your mission. Amen.

For Next Time

By working together with our brothers and sisters in Christ, we can do many things to support the church. Next week we'll discuss one way we can each individually help the church.

Church

Memory Verse

There were no needy persons among them. For from time to time those who owned lands or houses sold them, brought the money from the sales and put it at the apostles' feet, and it was distributed to anyone as he had need. Acts 4:34–35

40 We support the church with our tithes.

Before You Begin

- Read Malachi 3:10, Acts 2:42–47, Acts 4:34–35, and Philippians 4:19.
- Review the Teaching Points to familiarize yourself with the ideas to emphasize in this session.
- Read the session plan and select the elements that you will include.
- Choose a Bible memorization technique from those listed on page 122. Be sure to vary your teaching technique from session to session.
- If you choose to include a learning activity, gather the materials you will need.
  - For Activity 1 you will need a Monopoly™ game.
  - For Activity 2 you will need copies of the worksheet "Abundance," found on page 140, for each student.

Teaching Points

- The church is where we offer all of our resources to God.
- Tithes are gifts of our money that we give to God.
- We support the church with our tithes.

Say

Where does the church get money to pay the pastor, the heating and electric bills, and to provide emergency care for those in need? At some point, your parents have probably told you, "Money doesn't grow on trees." So where does the church get the money it needs to function?

The church gets its money from the people who attend it. The Bible calls the money that Christians give to the church a "tithe." It's one-tenth of what adults make in salaries and what you may make from chores and after-school jobs. This way, no matter how rich or how poor, Christians give the church the same percentage of their income.

While we certainly can't buy our way into heaven, we show that we love and trust God and believe in His work by giving one-tenth of everything we earn. One of the gifts that we offer God in thanksgiving is our money. We depend on money because it helps us get food, shelter, and everything we might need to live. Yet it can also be dangerous because it can be deceiving in its importance. Money doesn't do any good if it is hoarded or misused.

Sometimes the local church will use tithes to support the pastor or its ministry in the city where you live. Sometimes money from tithes will go all the way around the world to help missionaries build churches and serve others.

We support the church with our tithes.

Activity Options

Activity 1: *Monopoly™.* Using a Monopoly™ game board, show the students all money can buy. It buys land, possessions, fame, and more wealth. We encourage people to use their money to gain more money and more things, but God has instructed us to use our money for His purposes. This is why, as Christians, we gladly give at least one-tenth of what we earn back to Him and the Church.

Activity 2: *Abundance.* Use the worksheet on page 140 to help students see the blessings and resources they have available to them and how they can support others through their giving. Encourage them to do this activity with their family.

Action Point

You may not have a lot of money now, but it's important to develop the habit of giving God a portion of all your resources. Talk to your parents this week about how you can practice tithing.

Prayer

Lord, help us to serve and build up the church through our gifts and offerings of money. Teach us to use it wisely as we live and serve in this world. Amen.

For Next Time

Jesus had a mission. Next week we'll find out what that mission is and how we can be a part of it.

Church

Memory Verse

Therefore go and make disciples of all nations, baptizing them in the name of the Father and of the Son and of the Holy Spirit. Matthew 28:19

41 The church spreads the gospel around the world.

Before You Begin

- Read Isaiah 49:6, Mark 16:15–16, Luke 24:47–48, and Acts 1:8.
- Review the Teaching Points to familiarize yourself with the ideas to emphasize in this session.
- Read the session plan and select the elements that you will include.
- Choose a Bible memorization technique from those listed on page 122. Be sure to vary your teaching technique from session to session.
- If you choose to include a learning activity, gather the materials you will need.
  - For Activity 1 you will need several types of communication mediums including a newspaper, magazine, phone, walkie-talkie, radio, television, etc.
  - For Activity 2 you will need a map of the world and map pins.

Teaching Points

- Jesus commanded us to go and make disciples.
- The church spreads the gospel around the world.
- Jesus is the good news.

Say

Have you ever tried to keep a secret from someone you know? It's hard to keep something like that to ourselves. Thankfully, as Christians the most important thing we have to tell shouldn't be kept a secret. It's called the gospel. It really means good news. And news, especially good news, should be put in newspapers and magazines and on the radio and television. We share this good news with everyone we meet.

The best part of this good news is that we don't simply believe in a list of rules or a set of ideas. We all believe and follow a person who wants to be in relationship with us. That is Jesus Christ. This relationship is available to anyone who confesses their sins, receives the gift of forgiveness, and proclaims Jesus Christ as their savior. Anyone can have a relationship with Jesus that grows strong and healthy. We gather together each Sunday to celebrate that relationship.

But Jesus did not instruct us to celebrate the good news by ourselves. Sharing the good news around the world is one of the most important responsibilities Jesus gave the Church. He wants His family living here on earth to share the good news to those who have not heard it. The Church spreads the gospel around the world.

Activity Options

Activity 1: *Good news.* Have several types of communication mediums on display—newspapers, magazines, phone, walkie-talkie radio, television. These are all ways we hear news. Ask the students to discuss some ways they can share the good news about Jesus.

Activity 2: *Worldwide.* Ask your pastor or the missions committee to give you a list of the missionaries your local church supports and where they are in the world. Hang a map of the world on the wall, and place a map pin in each location to give students an idea of all the places the good news has already reached.

Action Point

We are all called to share the good news with others, but we don't have to leave our country to do it. Help spread the news about the gospel this week by telling one of your friends about Jesus.

Prayer

Lord, help us take the good news of Your life, death, and resurrection to the whole world. May our lives reflect Your love to everyone we meet. Amen.

For Next Time

Everyone who is a part of God's family is called to take the good news to the world. Next week we'll talk about a way we can help one another as we try to accomplish the mission Jesus gave us.

Church

Memory Verse

Be joyful always; pray continually; give thanks in all circumstances, for this is God's will for you in Christ Jesus. 1 Thessalonians 5:16–18

42 Christians pray for one another.

Before You Begin

- Read Romans 8:26–27, Ephesians 6:18, 1 Timothy 2:8, and James 5:14–16.
- Review the Teaching Points to familiarize yourself with the ideas to emphasize in this session.
- Read the session plan and select the elements that you will include.
- Choose a Bible memorization technique from those listed on page 122. Be sure to vary your teaching technique from session to session.
- If you choose to include a learning activity, gather the materials you will need.
  - For Activity 1 you will need an index card and markers for each student.
  - For Activity 2 you will need a hula-hoop.

Teaching Points

- Jesus' prayer is our example of how to pray for others.
- Intercessory prayer is praying for one another.
- Christians pray for one another.

Say

A little boy was overheard praying: "Lord, if you can't make me a better boy, don't worry about it. I'm having a real good time like I am!"

Little children can pray the funniest prayers. But as we grow older most of us realize that our communication with God through prayer is important because it helps us have a strong, healthy relationship with Him. We don't have friends just so they will give us things we want. We don't just pray to God for things we want. We pray to God because we love Him and we want to please Him.

What pleases Him and shows that we love Him is our concern and love for other people. But we don't just pray for our relatives and close friends. As Christians we pray for everyone, including people who don't like us and people we don't know. We pray for others because we know how much we need God as our creator and protector, and we want others to understand the love God has for them as well.

Praying for everyone can be a really hard thing to do—especially if we are praying for someone who isn't very nice. That's why Christians pray together. We have other brothers and sisters in Christ who can help us and pray for us even when we don't feel like praying. They pray with us and for us because we're all trying to become more like Him. Christians pray for one another.

Activity Options

Activity 1: *Praying together.* Guided prayers can be helpful for people uncomfortable or unfamiliar with prayer. Have each child write the name of a person they want to pray for on an index card. They may or may not choose to write why. Collect the cards. Then redistribute among the children. Begin the prayer, "Dear Lord, we thank You for hearing our prayers. Today we want to pray for those around us." Have each child say, "I want to pray for (*names the person on the card*) today. This person needs prayer for (*if a request is provided on the card*)." Conclude the prayer, "Thank you, God, for hearing each one of our prayers. Help us this week as we continue to pray for each one of these people. Amen."

Activity 2: *Hug 'em in.* Place a hula hoop on the floor. Students must try to fit as many people as possible inside the hula hoop without stepping outside the hoop. Ask the children how this is like prayer for one another. Emphasize that we all share the same mission, and that we should support one another through prayer.

Action Point

Prayer is central to keeping a good relationship with God and supporting the Church as it carries out its mission. How often do you pray for other brothers and sisters in Christ?

Prayer

Lord, today we pray especially for our brothers and sisters in Christ. Help us to know you are near as we learn to become more like You. Amen.

For Next Time

This week we talked about praying with our brothers and sisters in Christ. Come next week to learn about another activity Christians do together.

Church

Memory Verse
They devoted themselves to the apostles' teaching and to the fellowship, to the breaking of bread and to prayer. Acts 2:42

43 Christians meet together for worship.

Before You Begin

- Read Acts 2:42–47, Colossians 3:16, and Hebrews 10:25.
- Review the Teaching Points to familiarize yourself with the ideas to emphasize in this session.
- Read the session plan and select the elements that you will include.
- Choose a Bible memorization technique from those listed on page 122. Be sure to vary your teaching technique from session to session.
- If you choose to include a learning activity, gather the materials you will need.
  - For Activity 1 you will need some soft worship music and candles or incense.

Teaching Points

- Worship includes preparing our hearts, gathering together with brothers and sisters in Christ, and responding to the Word of God.
- Worship is about God, not us.
- Christians meet together for worship.

Say

Often we think of worship as simply a routine of singing, prayer, offering, and preaching. But worshipping God is so much more than that. Worship involves putting our faith into practice and celebrating being children of God.

In fact, worship takes a lot of preparation. If you ever had the chance to meet a famous person like the President of the United States or a movie star, you would want to be prepared by thinking about what you should say or do when you were around them. But God is more important than anyone we could ever meet, and we meet Him every week in worship! Before we meet with him, it's important that we also take time to prepare. We do this by praying that our hearts and minds will be open, so we can hear what God has to say to us during worship.

After we prepare, it's important that we spend time worshipping with other members of God's family. Christians meet together for worship. While it's possible to worship God by yourself, it's hard to be a Christian by yourself. That's one reason why Christians pray for one another. We need other people because we are all trying to do the same thing—become more like our Father. Worshipping together helps us focus on God and hear what God is saying to all of us. We tell the story of our salvation together so that when we leave our time of worship, we can tell it to others. When we work at this together, we can see God working in us.

Finally, as we worship and listen for God's word to us, we respond. We might eat the Lord's Supper, confess something we've done wrong, sing praises, or pray. Whatever we do, we do as brothers and sisters in Christ. Christians meet together for worship.

Activity Options

Activity 1: *Preparation.* Worship usually requires some time to quiet our minds and our hearts before we are ready to hear God's Word. Provide a quiet time of worship preparation before leaving the classroom. Play some soft worship music a few minutes prior to dismissing the students to the worship service. Burn incense or a scented candle. Perhaps you can offer a guided prayer or read Psalm 117 to help students focus on the worship they will experience.

Activity 2: *Prayer*. Take time to guide the students in a prayer for the leaders of your church's worship service. Explain that this can also be part of preparation for worship.

Action Point

Do you usually take time to prepare to worship with your brothers and sisters in Christ? Take time this week to prepare your hearts for the next time you will gather together with others to worship God.

Prayer

Lord, as we worship You, help us to focus our hearts and our minds solely upon You. We give You praise for who You are and thank You for the love You show us each day. Amen.

For Next Time

If we can't see God, and Jesus is in heaven, how can God help us? Next week we will learn about the gift Jesus gave to help us as we wait for His return.

The Christian Life

44 God sent the Holy Spirit to help us.

Before You Begin

- Read Joel 2:28–29, Acts 1:8, Romans 8:26, 2 Corinthians 1:21–22, and Galatians 4:6.
- Review the Teaching Points to familiarize yourself with the ideas to emphasize in this session.
- Read the session plan and select the elements that you will include.
- Choose a Bible memorization technique from those listed on page 122. Be sure to vary your teaching technique from session to session.
- If you choose to include a learning activity, gather the materials you will need.
  - For Activity 1 you will need a candle, matches, a small fan, and a pitcher of water.
  - For Activity 2 you will need construction paper, red, orange, yellow, blue and white tissue papers, scissors, a hole punch, a stapler, and yarn for each student.

Teaching Points

- The Holy Spirit is the third person in the Trinity.
- God sent the Holy Spirit to help the Church.
- God sent the Holy Spirit to help us.

Say

After Jesus gave the Church its mission to carry on His work of salvation here on earth, He returned to heaven. Thankfully, He did not leave us alone. God sent the Holy Spirit to help us carry out His important mission. Because the Spirit's mission is so connected with ours, we can know that He is always near and available to us. Like the Father and the Son, the Spirit has always existed. He was present with the Father and the Son at Creation. The Spirit can be described as wind or as breath, but He can also be thought of as a comforter and a helper for us.

98

When the Church began, the Holy Spirit was present in a special way. The people who were there that day saw the Holy Spirit as a tongue of fire. While fire can be dangerous, it can also clean forests and help trees to spread their seeds. The Holy Spirit, who is present in our lives, cleanses and purifies our hearts and our minds. He helps us as we listen for God to speak to us, and He then helps us respond to it. In fact, even today as we worship together, the Holy Spirit is present and is helping us to love one another. God sent the Holy Spirit to help us.

Activity Options

Activity 1: *Elements.* The Holy Spirit is often associated with elemental aspects of nature, such as fire, wind, and water. As you discuss the Spirit's different qualities, illustrate them with a candle, a fan, and a pitcher of water.

Activity 2: *Wind of the Spirit.* Make a windsock using colored tissue paper and construction paper. Cut and tear strips of all the colors of tissue paper (red, orange, yellow, blue and white) and staple along one long edge of construction paper. Staple or glue construction paper into a cylinder. Hole punch two holes on one end of tube on opposite sides. Thread yarn through the holes and hang outside. When the class is finished making the windsocks, discuss once again the ways in which the Holy Spirit is like the wind.

Action Point

The Holy Spirit is available to us whenever we call for Him. What concerns do you have that the Holy Spirit can help you with? Ask Him for His help.

Prayer

Lord, thank You for sending Your Holy Spirit to help us and sense your presence among us. We ask for His guidance as we continue to walk with You each day. Amen.

For Next Time

When we are looking for answers to hard questions, we have the Holy Spirit with us to help us. Next week, we'll learn how the Holy Spirit helps us by showing us truth.

The Christian Life

Memory Verse

And I will ask the Father, and he will give you another Counselor to be with you forever-the Spirit of truth. The world cannot accept him, because it neither sees him nor knows him. But you know him, for he lives with you and will be in you. John 14:16 &17

45 The Holy Spirit helps us understand the truth.

Before You Begin

■ Read John 14:16–17, John 16:13–15, Romans 8:16, 1 Corinthians 2:10–13, and 2 Thessalonians 2:13.

■ Review the Teaching Points to familiarize yourself with the ideas to emphasize in this session.

■ Read the session plan and select the elements that you will include.

■ Choose a Bible memorization technique from those listed on page 122. Be sure to vary your teaching technique from session to session.

■ If you choose to include a learning activity, gather the materials you will need.

• For Activity 1 you will need glass cleaner and a picture frame with the glass only (no photo or backboard) smeared with dirt and grime.

• For Activity 2 you will need to copy "Fruit Jumble," found on page 141, and distribute to each student.

Teaching Points

■ The Holy Spirit helps us understand the truth.
■ Jesus is the truth.
■ The Spirit of God lives in us as we become more Christ-like.

Say

If you've ever tried to look through a window that is smudged and dirty, you know how hard it is to see out. The dust blocks any clear view. As we think of the Holy Spirit as a cleansing power in our lives, we can understand how the Spirit helps us understand the truth.

When we talk about truth, we mean more than just facts or even beliefs. Our truth is a person, and His name is Jesus Christ. Our focus as children of God should always be on Him. But sometimes our view of Him can be ruined by our disobedience, pride, and independence. We may not have a clear picture of Jesus. But the Spirit is always pointing to God. He reminds us of Jesus' life, death, and resurrection—the mission He completed while He was here on earth. The Spirit reminds us of how Jesus spoke and acted so that we may become more like Him. The Spirit helps us clear away everything that might get between God and us. When the Spirit is near, we are ready to hear and respond to what God wants us to be and to do. This is part of what it means to become more like Christ. The Holy Spirit helps us understand the truth.

Activity Options

Activity 1: *Clear view.* Use a picture frame with the glass only (no photo, back board) smeared with dirt and grime. Use glass cleaner as an illustration of the Holy Spirit's cleansing work in our lives.

Activity 2: *Fruit Jumble.* Copy worksheet found on page 141 and distribute to each student. In small groups have the students unscramble the Fruits of the Spirit and then match each fruit to their definition and scripture reference. Share with the class how The Holy Spirit produces fruit in our lives-Fruit of the Spirit.

Action Point

Jesus' life and ministry is a guide for how we should live our lives, and it is an example of living out the truth in the world. Trust the Holy Spirit to give you wisdom as you seek His truth.

Prayer

Lord, we pray that Your Spirit would help us as we seek and try to understand Your truth. You have shown us what truth is through Your Son, Jesus Christ. Help us now to live this truth out each day. Amen.

For Next Time

We not only know and understand truth, but we can also act upon it. We will talk about how the Holy Spirit helps us obey God next week.

The Christian Life

46 The Holy Spirit helps us obey God.

Before You Begin

- Read Romans 8:1–17, Ephesians 3:14–19.
- Review the Teaching Points to familiarize yourself with the ideas to emphasize in this session.
- Read the session plan and select the elements that you will include.
- Choose a Bible memorization technique from those listed on page 122. Be sure to vary your teaching technique from session to session.
- If you choose to include a learning activity, gather the materials you will need.
  - For Activity 1 you will need a picture of a car engine.
  - For Activity 2 you will need blindfolds for each student, a bowl, and paper.

Teaching Points

- We must know and obey God.
- The Holy Spirit helps us obey God.
- Obeying God means loving God and loving others.

Say

Do you know how a car works? You may see your mom put the key in the ignition to turn it on. You feel the wheels turn as you back out of the driveway. You're glad that there are brakes that help you stop at a stop sign. You ride in a car every day, but you probably don't know how a car turns on, moves, or stops. You know enough to trust that it will get you where you want to go. There's a difference between doing something and actually knowing why or how you're doing it.

Sometimes trusting God is a lot like driving a car. We don't completely understand how God works, or why he sometimes asks us to do certain things, but with the help of the Holy Spirit, we obey Him. The Holy Spirit helps us not only to hear God speak and understand Him, but also to obey what He asks us to do.

Jesus gave His followers many instructions like feed the hungry, heal the sick, and preach the word. These are all important and specific ways we can show God how much we love Him. But Jesus also simplified all of the instructions He ever gave into two simple commands. He told His followers to love Him and to love others. It may sound simple, but obeying those commands can often be difficult. Loving God and loving others means we may need to do things that are not always easy or comfortable for us, such as forgiving people who have hurt us. That's why we need the Holy Spirit to help us obey God.

Activity Options

Activity 1: *Obedience working.* Help students understand that obedience does not always require complete knowledge. It requires trust. Show the students a picture of a car engine to show the intricate system that makes a car run. Point out that we don't need to know every aspect of car mechanics to ride in or drive a car. In the same way, we don't need to fully understand God to trust that we should obey His commands. The Holy Spirit helps us to obey God when we don't understand why He's commanding us to do certain things.

Activity 2: *Blind obedience.* Trust is an important aspect of obedience. This game requires trust and following directions to complete the task. Line students up for a relay and blindfold each of them. Write tasks on pieces of paper, and place them in a bowl for each team. Tasks might include picking up a specific object, erasing part of the chalkboard, etc. Designate one person from each team to draw a paper from the bowl and read the task aloud. Since players cannot see, each director must call out directions for the tasks. The first team to go through their line wins.

Action Point

Obedience to God shows you are a child of God. Is there something that God has been asking you to do? Ask the Holy Spirit to help you obey.

Prayer

Lord, we pray that Your Spirit would help us as we seek to understand and obey Your will. Help us to do Your will in loving You and loving others. Amen.

For Next Time

One way we can obey God is to help others. Next week we will talk about how the Holy Spirit enables us to do this.

The Christian Life

Memory Verse

Keep watch over yourselves and all the flock of which the Holy Spirit has made you overseers. Be shepherds of the church of God, which he bought with his own blood. Acts 20:28

The Holy Spirit helps us serve others.

Before You Begin

- Read John 13:1–16 and 1 Corinthians 12:4–11.
- Review the Teaching Points to familiarize yourself with the ideas to emphasize in this session.
- Read the session plan and select the elements that you will include.
- Choose a Bible memorization technique from those listed on page 122. Be sure to vary your teaching technique from session to session.
- If you choose to include a learning activity, gather the materials you will need.
  - For Activity 1 you will need a basin, water, and soap.
  - For Activity 2 you will need paper, tape, and glue.

Teaching Points

- The Holy Spirit helps us serve others.
- We become more like Jesus as we serve others.
- Serving others helps the Church fulfill its mission.

Say

How would you feel if the President of the United States came to your house and cleaned your bathroom and cooked dinner for your family? You might feel awkward because someone in such a high position is serving you. Jesus' disciples were put in a very similar situation when one day Jesus decided to wash their feet. This act of service was usually only done by the slaves or servants. Although He was a king and their leader, He chose to take the role of a servant. Because of Jesus' example, we can know what it means to humbly serve others.

Serving others is part of the mission that Jesus gave to the Church. He sent the Holy Spirit to help us serve others. The Holy Spirit has given us talents and abilities to be used in service to others. We offer these things to the Church so it can fulfill its mission. The Holy Spirit also helps us by giving us special gifts, like the ability to be encouraging or a good listener. These are things we can do to help serve people and keep the Church healthy.

It's often difficult to know who we can help and how, but the Holy Spirit helps us by guiding us to people whom we can serve and by telling us how we can best help them. The Holy Spirit helps us serve others.

Activity Options

Activity 1: *Foot washing.* Illustrate the undignified action of washing feet by asking your students if you can wash their feet. After you have washed their feet, ask if they would like to wash one of their classmate's feet.

Activity 2: *Serving chain.* By participating in this project, students can learn how their acts of service can edify and build up the church. Cut strips of paper, and on one side of each one, write a way the children can serve in the local church. Examples include making cards for shut-ins, folding bulletins, sweeping floors, washing windows, or helping to set up classrooms. Loop each strip to form a paper chain. Have each child take a link from the chain and do the service sometime during the next week.

Action Point

Ask for the Holy Spirit to give you directions concerning whom you can serve this week.

Prayer

Lord, we pray that Your Spirit would help us as we seek to serve others. As brothers and sisters in Christ, help us to serve through the gifts and abilities the Holy Spirit has given us. Amen.

For Next Time

Over the last few weeks we've discussed the many ways in which the Holy Spirit helps us. Come next week to find out about something else God has given us to help us grow stronger.

The Christian Life

Memory Verse

How can a young man keep his way pure? By living according to your word. I seek you with all my heart; do not let me stray from your commands. I have hidden your words in my heart that I might not sin against you. Psalm 119:9-11

48 We grow stronger by learning God's Word.

Before You Begin

- Read Psalm 119:28, Proverbs 6:23, Romans 15:4, Ephesians 1:17–21, and 1 Peter 4:11.
- Review the Teaching Points to familiarize yourself with the ideas to emphasize in this session.
- Read the session plan and select the elements that you will include.
- Choose a Bible memorization technique from those listed on page 122. Be sure to vary your teaching technique from session to session.
- If you choose to include a learning activity, gather the materials you will need.
  - For Activity 1 you will need a bottle of vitamin C, or foods such as strawberries, oranges, and hot peppers that contain a lot of vitamin C.

Teaching Points

- Scripture helps us in our relationship with God.
- We grow stronger by learning God's Word.
- When we learn about Jesus, we have a pattern to follow.

Say

Do you ever find yourself finishing your best friends' sentences? Or do you always know how they will answer your questions before you even ask them? You're able to do this because you've spent a lot of time with your friends and know them very well. God wants us to know Him just as well, if not better, than we know our friends. One way we can have this kind of strong relationship with Him is by reading Scripture, which is God's story.

When we want to have a strong relationship with God, it means that we want to know what God's will is so that we can do it. We can find out what God's will is for us, or how he wants us to live, by reading the Bible. Scripture also tells us stories about God and His relationships with other faithful people. By reading about these people, we can better understand how God wants to relate to us, His children. As we learn about God and His will for us, our relationship with Him will be strengthened. We grow stronger by learning God's Word.

Scripture is that important because it strengthens the body of Christ, the Church. Just as our own bodies are strengthened and protected by different vitamins and minerals that we eat and drink throughout the day, the body of Christ is strengthened and protected by Scripture. God's Word is like vitamin C for the Body of Christ. It supports and fortifies everything from the feet to the forehead through its teaching, correction, and wisdom. As we strengthen ourselves on God's Word, we are able to support others and resist temptation. In the Bible, we learn that when Jesus was tempted by the devil, He used Scripture to remain strong and resist. This shows us the strength and power of Scripture in our lives. We grow by learning God's Word.

Activity Options

Activity 1: *Vitamins.* Show a bottle of vitamin C or foods such as strawberries, oranges, and hot peppers that contain a lot of vitamin C to talk about how vitamins strengthen and protect our bodies. Compare the effects of vitamin C on our bodies to the effects of Scripture on the body of Christ.

Activity 2: *Memorization.* One way to allow Scripture to strengthen us is to memorize it. Use several of the methods listed on page 122 to help the students learn the memory verse for today. If time allows, review some of the memory verses they have learned from previous weeks.

Action Point

How often do you read your Bible? Ask God to help you to read Scripture every day so your relationship with Him can grow stronger.

Prayer

Lord, help us as we hide Your words in our hearts. Make them come alive to us. Then help us to live out those words of life by loving and serving You. Amen.

For Next Time

There are certain things we do to honor God—like reading the Bible—that show Him how much we want to have a relationship with Him. Next week we'll talk about something else that strengthens our relationship with God.

The Christian Life

Memory Verse

But those who hope in the Lord will renew their strength. They will soar on wings like eagles; they will run and not grow weary, they will walk and not be faint. Isaiah 40:31

49 We grow stronger by praying to God.

Before You Begin

- Read 2 Chronicles 7:14, Psalm 46:1, Psalm 118:14, and Isaiah 40:29–31.
- Review the Teaching Points to familiarize yourself with the ideas to emphasize in this session.
- Read the session plan and select the elements that you will include.
- Choose a Bible memorization technique from those listed on page 122. Be sure to vary your teaching technique from session to session.
- If you choose to include a learning activity, gather the materials you will need.
  - For Activity 1 you will need black construction paper and crayons.
  - For Activity 2 you will need construction paper, markers, and scissors.

Teaching Points

- Prayer strengthens our relationship with God.
- Prayer was a source of strength for Jesus.
- We grow stronger by praying to God.

Say

If you wanted to strengthen your relationship with one of your friends, how would you do it? Perhaps you would start to spend more time with your friend or talk to him or her more often. We can strengthen our relationship with God in a very similar way. We do this by praying, or talking to God. In prayer, we can go directly to God and share our needs and desires with Him. But prayer doesn't only involve us talking to God; it also involves God speaking to us. As we communicate with Him, He will give us wisdom and understanding and strengthen us to do His will. We grow stronger by praying to God.

Jesus knew that prayer was important, and He used it as a source of strength. While He was in the wilderness, Jesus spent most of His time in prayer, talking with the Father. He was physically weak from fasting.

He needed the strength of prayer to resist the temptations of Satan. We depend on God to protect us from temptations as well. Our strongest defense is through regular prayer. We grow stronger by praying to God.

Prayer not only strengthens you, but it also strengthens the entire Church. Prayer reaches to every part of the body of Christ, protecting and supporting it. We grow stronger by praying to God.

Activity Options

Activity 1: *Got prayer?* Have each student draw a self-portrait on a sheet of black construction paper. Then, with a white crayon, have them draw a milk mustache on their upper lip. Discuss the parallels between milk and prayer: Milk makes our bones and bodies strong. Prayer is like milk for our souls. It strengthens our relationship with God and others. Hang the pictures on a bulletin board, or let the students take their art home as a reminder to pray.

Activity 2: *Praying Hands.* This exercise helps remind students to pray for others. Each child begins by tracing their hand with a marker. The thumb reminds us to pray for friends and family. The index finger helps us pray for those who point us to God. Because the middle finger is the tallest, we pray for leaders in our country, state, and town. The ring finger is the weakest, so we pray for those who are less fortunate than we are. The pinkie finger reminds us to pray for ourselves. Have the students label each finger, and then cut out the hand. Encourage them to use the hand as a reminder to pray for people this week. (Activity adapted from *Before and After Easter* by Debbie Trafton O'Neal).

Action Point

Prayer strengthens our relationship with God. He desires to talk with us every day about what's going on in our life. What do you need to talk about with God today?

Prayer

Lord, we pray for Your strength and protection as we live each day as Your children. Help us to listen for Your words of strength and encouragement whenever they are spoken. Amen.

For Next Time

Prayer is a very important aspect of the Christian life. Next week we'll talk about another important aspect: helping people who are in need.

The Christian Life

Memory Verse

All the believers were together and had everything in common. Selling their possessions and goods, they gave to anyone as he had need. Acts 2:44–45

50 Christians help those in need.

Before You Begin

- Read Isaiah 58: 6–12 and Luke 10:25–37.
- Review the Teaching Points to familiarize yourself with the ideas to emphasize in this session.
- Read the session plan and select the elements that you will include.
- Choose a Bible memorization technique from those listed on page 122. Be sure to vary your teaching technique from session to session.
- If you choose to include a learning activity, gather the materials you will need.
  - For Activity 1 you will need paper, crayons, and scissors.

Teaching Points

- Christians help and care for all of their neighbors.
- We express our love for others through acts of compassion.
- Christians help those in need.

Say

We know that Jesus showed us how to serve others so that the Church could be strong and healthy. Serving people by using the gifts and talents God has given us helps to encourage people and build them up spiritually. The mission that Jesus gave us involves being sensitive to all kinds of needs and being willing to use our gifts to help people. Christians help those in need.

We live in a world full of people with needs. Many people have no money or shelter, little food or clothing, poor health, and few companions. Jesus wants us to serve everyone, no matter who they are or what they have done. Jesus forgave the sins of those who were rejected by society. He touched the widow, the orphan, the handicapped, and even the disobedient. He also healed them of sickness, blindness, and their feelings of worthlessness. He still loves everyone and offers to all the gift of forgiveness and eternal life through the giving of His own body.

Jesus set an example for us by helping those in need. Healing the visible needs of people was just as important as healing their spiritual needs. The physical healings reflected the spiritual healing that was going on inside of them. If we are Christ's body in the world today, then part of our responsibility includes acts of compassion for those in need. Christians help those in need.

Activity Options

Activity 1: *Hands of service.* Have each child trace their hands on a sheet of paper. This represents their hands in service to their family and friends. Outline the hand in another color. This represents their service to their local church. Draw a third outline around the hand. This represents their service to the world—people they don't know and those in need. Have them cut out the hand to serve as a reminder of the responsibility they have to all of their neighbors.

Activity 2: *Service in action.* Find someone in your congregation such as an elderly or chronically ill person, whom your students can serve. The class might choose to make a card, prepare food, mow the lawn, or simply visit the person in need.

Action Point

What kind of spiritual and physical needs do you see around you? Is someone sick? Hungry? Lonely? How can you serve them this week?

Prayer

Lord, we pray today for eyes that see the needs of this world, hearts that love those who are in need, and hands that are willing to serve them. Amen.

For Next Time

Throughout Jesus' life, He served people in many different ways, often by fulfilling their physical and spiritual needs. Next week we'll talk about how Jesus continues to serve us today by fulfilling our need for hope and courage.

The Christian Life

Memory Verse

I have told you these things, so that in me you may have peace. In this world you will have trouble. But take heart! I have overcome the world! John 16:33

51 Living for Jesus makes life better.

Before You Begin

- Read John 16:31–33, Romans 8:28, 2 Corinthians 4:7–11, and Philippians 4:13.
- Review the Teaching Points to familiarize yourself with the ideas to emphasize in this session.
- Read the session plan and select the elements that you will include.
- Choose a Bible memorization technique from those listed on page 122. Be sure to vary your teaching technique from session to session.
- If you choose to include a learning activity, gather the materials you will need.
  - For Activity 1 you will need copies of the worksheet "Word Jumble" found on page 142 for each student.
  - For Activity 2 you will need aluminum foil, construction paper, a heart pattern, a clothespin with a spring, and a sticker that says, "Jesus gives me hope and courage" (print on address labels) for each student.

Teaching Points

- Living for Jesus makes life better.
- Hope and courage is found in living for Jesus.

Say

Marathon runners have a very long and difficult task before them as they train for their race. They may prepare by lifting weights, doing aerobic workouts, and running up and down stairs, so their muscles, heart, bones, and mind are ready for the test of endurance and strength.

Athletes or anyone who has a very difficult task to complete often use words like "courage" and "hope." Christians also use these two words often because, like running long race, living the Christian life can be very difficult.

Sometimes it seems like the world does not want us to accomplish the mission Jesus has given us. Having a relationship with God does make life better, but it does not guarantee that we will avoid hardship and persecution here on earth. But God has given us the Holy Spirit, who is always with us, comforting us during difficult times. God also gave us someone who gives us hope and courage to carry out our mission in the world. Our hope is in Jesus Christ, who has promised to return someday. Our courage is found in living each day, knowing that we can trust in God, who loves and cares for us. With hope and courage from the Holy Spirit, we can live joyfully for God and others. Living for Jesus makes life better.

Activity Options

Activity 1: *Word jumble*. Using the worksheet found on page 142, have students unscramble the words in the puzzle to learn more about hope and courage.

Activity 2: *Courage badges*. We often honor people like firefighters, policemen, and soldiers for the courage they demonstrate. But Christians show courage as well. Give each child a piece of aluminum foil, a piece of construction paper, a heart pattern, a clothespin with a spring, and a sticker that says, "Jesus gives me hope and courage." (You can print these words on address labels to make stickers.) Students trace the heart pattern onto aluminum foil and a piece of construction paper, and then cut out both. Paste the aluminum foil and construction paper hearts to each other. Place the sticker on the front of the heart. Attach heart to clothespin. Students can wear their badges on their shirts.

Action Point

How does knowing and believing in Jesus' life, death, and resurrection give you hope and courage?

Prayer

Lord, thank You for the hope and courage that You have given to us through the presence of Your Holy Spirit. Help us to live in this hope and courage each day as we seek to love You and others. Amen.

For Next Time

We've talked about the hope and courage that Jesus gives us. Next week, we'll talk about Jesus' promise of eternal life as something we can all look forward to.

The Christian Life

Memory Verse

And if I go and prepare a place for you, I will come back and take you to be with me that you also may be where I am. John 14:3

 52 **Jesus will come back and take us to heaven.**

Before You Begin

■ Read John 6:40, Thessalonians 4:16–17, and Revelation 21.
■ Review the Teaching Points to familiarize yourself with the ideas to emphasize in this session.
■ Read the session plan and select the elements that you will include.
■ Choose a Bible memorization technique from those listed on page 122. Be sure to vary your teaching technique from session to session.
■ If you choose to include a learning activity, gather the materials you will need.
  • For Activity 1 you will need one fresh egg and one hard-boiled egg.
  • For Activity 2 you will need various items from the classroom and two laundry baskets.

Teaching Points

■ Jesus promises us eternal life.
■ As Jesus is preparing a place for us, we must prepare our hearts for Him.
■ Jesus will come back and take us to heaven.

Say

When we confess our sins and declare Jesus as Lord, we receive the promise of eternal life. Even now Jesus is getting ready to return to earth. When Jesus comes, He will raise us from the dead, just like He rose from the tomb. Once He returns, He will take us to live with Him forever in heaven. We will not be angels or little gods, but we will be completely restored to what we were always supposed to be. Like Adam and Eve before they sinned, we will be able to talk and walk with God in a perfect relationship with Him. We will be in the presence of God with all the angels and all the faithful people who have lived before and after us. Together, we will worship and praise God forever.

Jesus promised that He is preparing a place for us in heaven, so it's important that we also prepare to be with Him. One way that we can prepare to be with Jesus is to worship Him here on earth. By constantly being in prayer, we can know what it's like to constantly be in His presence, just like we will be in heaven. We practice preparing our hearts for Jesus because He will come back and take us to heaven.

Activity Options

Activity 1: *The transformed egg.* This analogy can help students understand the transformation we go through in the resurrection. Show a fresh egg. It is made up of a shell, a yolk, and clear fluid. You can see that when we break this egg it runs all over. Show the hard boiled egg. This egg has gone through a transformation. It's still an egg. It has a shell, white stuff, and a yolk. Yet when broken, we can see that it remains whole. That is similar to what our bodies will be like. We will still be ourselves, but we will be changed and made completely whole.

Activity 2: *Get ready room relay.* Gather various things from around the room and divide them evenly into two baskets. You can use crayons, paper, a cloth or clothes, toys, etc. Divide students into two teams. The first person in line must run to the basket, pick up an item, and return it to its place in the room neatly and correctly. The first team to empty its basket wins.

Action Point

Are you looking forward to Jesus' return? How are you preparing your heart for eternity with Him?

Prayer

Lord, as we celebrate and live in the knowledge of Your life, death and resurrection, we look forward to Your return. Help us to live each day expecting to see You. Amen.

Developmental Characteristics of Elementary Students

Children develop quickly through the elementary school years. Their size, social skills, self-image, and intellectual depth change dramatically during the ages from six to ten years old. Children learn to read and thus open up to enormous opportunities for learning. They begin to think logically, connect items, and grasp time. Children gain greater independence and, although they still want to please their parents and teachers, begin to feel the pull of social acceptance. These are the years of industry and, as Erik Erikson points out, can lead to feelings of inferiority or incompetence. It is crucial to help these children step into adolescence feeling confident about themselves and their abilities.

Mental

Children begin to think logically in a concrete manner; they can grasp symbolism and time and understand cause and effect. At this age, they have an enormous capability to memorize and remember. Imagination becomes internalized.

Social

Elementary children want to meet the expectations of everyone, parents, teachers, and friends. They strive for fairness and friendship. At this age, they understand that people have value, and they can differentiate right from wrong.

Emotional

Elementary children struggle for independence while longing for love and affection. The difference between the ways boys and girls express affection begins to become apparent. They enjoy humor, have difficulty controlling anger, and need a structured routine. This is the age of self-awareness.

Spiritual

Children are in the story phase of faith development. They begin to see God working in the everyday aspects of their lives. Church is viewed positively and is a place they want to be.

Physical

Elementary children generally grow two inches and gain six pounds each year. Growth occurs in "spurts." Pre-puberty physical signs begin to appear, although there are significant differences in development. Athletically, they develop speed and accuracy.

Multiple Intelligence

Dr. Howard Gardner from Harvard University developed a theory that states that we all learn through eight different forms of intelligence. Traditional education generally teaches only two forms. The goal of the teacher is to implement as many of these forms of teaching as possible into the classroom setting.

- Verbal/Linguistic—Learn through hearing stories, reading, writing, and memorizing.

- Logical/Mathematical—Learn with numbers, ask many questions, think logically, need organization, solve problems easily.

- Visual/Spatial—Learn through seeing drawings, pictures, colorful bulletin boards, and by painting, drawing, and sculpting. These kids love videos and making art projects.

- Musical/Rhythmic—Learn through music, sound, rhythm, and pitch.

- Bodily/Kinesthetic—Learn by playing games, moving around, acting out events.

- Introspective—These children are very reflective, self-motivated, and enjoy time alone. They will learn through one-on-one interaction, quiet reflection, and independent study. They are often mislabeled as "shy."

- Interpersonal—These children are talkative, friendly, and outgoing. They learn best in group settings and enjoy social times and parties.

- Naturalist—Learn through being outdoors and experiencing nature. They enjoy field trips, a class pet, and classifying information.

By being able to recognize how each of your students learns best, you can better understand how to keep them active learners rather than disruptive bystanders.

Learning Styles

When developing your lesson, you need to be conscious of the following four learning styles and try to incorporate as many as you can into each lesson. People generally tend to teach toward their own learning style. Constant teaching using only one style will encourage discipline problems within the classroom.

Visual Learners

Visual learners need to see what you're talking about. Include bulletin boards, charts, graphs, pictures, and lots of color.

Auditory Learners

These children learn through hearing. They will respond well to verbal directions, use music, and even the "learning noise" in the classroom. They might need to hear their own voice in order to learn. Understand that sound is comforting to them.

Tactile Learners

Tactile learners need to touch and feel what they are learning. Having something they can hold onto or make with their hands while learning will enhance their experience.

Kinesthetic Learners

These children learn through using their whole self. These kids need movement and activity. Include large muscle activities and drama to encourage them to learn.

The best way to determine the learning style of a child is to observe them in the classroom. See what activities and learning experiences they favor. If a student is having a behavior problem, try to include a tactile or kinesthetic experience and see if they respond positively.

References

Henley, Karyn (1997). Child-Sensitive Teaching, Cincinnati, Ohio: Standard Publishing.

Keener, Patricia A., M.D. (2001). Caring for Kids. Indianapolis, Indiana: James Whitcomb Riley Memorial Association.

Schaefer, Charles E. (2000). Ages and Stages, New York, Chichester, Weinheim, Brisbane, Singapore, Toronto: John Wiley & Sons, Inc.

Elementary Assessment Tool

1. **How many gods are there?**

   There is only one God.

2. **What is greater than God?**

   Nothing is greater than God.

3. **What did God make the world from?**

   God made the world from nothing.

4. **How did God create the world?**

   God created the world by speaking it into existence.

5. **What part of creation does God love?**

   God loves all of creation.

6. **Which words describe God?**

   God is perfect.
   God is fair.
   God is faithful.

7. **Where can we see God?**

   We can see God in creation and history.
   We can see God in Scripture and in Jesus.

8. **Where is God?**

   God is everywhere all the time.

9. **How much does God know?**

   God knows everything.
   God knows me.

10. **How can we talk to God?**

    We talk to God through prayer.

11. What is the Bible?

The Bible is God's written Word.

12. What does the Bible tell us?

The Bible tells us who God is.
The Bible tells us what God has done.

13. What do we know about the Bible?

The Bible is true.
The Bible never changes.

14. Who were you created to be like?

I was created in God's image.

15. What does God think about you?

God thinks I am valuable and unique.

16. Who is responsible for your choices?

I am responsible for my choices.
God gives me freedom to make choices.

17. What should your thoughts and actions be?

My thoughts and actions should be pure.
My thoughts and actions should reflect God's will.

18. Who is Jesus?

Jesus is the Son of God.

19. Is Jesus God or human?

Jesus is both God and human.

20. Did Jesus ever sin?

Jesus never sinned.

21. Was Jesus ever tempted?

Jesus was tempted, but He did not sin.

22. Why did Jesus come to earth?

Jesus came to earth to be our savior.

23. What is a savior?

A savior is someone who rescues you, or saves you from something.

24. How did Jesus become our savior?

Jesus died on the cross for our sins.

25. What happened to Jesus after He died on the cross?

God raised Jesus from the dead.

26. Who has sinned?

Everyone has sinned.

27. What does sin do?

Sin separates us from God.

28. What did God do about our sin?

God sent Jesus to forgive us for our sins.

29. What can we do about our sin?

We can ask forgiveness for our sins.
We can stop sinning.

30. What will God do if we ask forgiveness for our sins?

He will forgive us of our sins.

31. What happens when we are forgiven?

When we are forgiven, we become part of God's family.
When we are forgiven, we are given the gift of living for eternity in heaven.

32. Who makes up the Church?

The Church is made up of people who believe in Jesus Christ.

33. What does baptism represent?

Baptism represents our new life in Jesus Christ.

34. What does the Lord's Supper represent?

The Lord's Supper represents Christ's sacrifice for us.

35. What can we do at church?

We can help others at church.
We can support the church with our tithes.
We can worship together at church.

36. Who is our helper?

The Holy Spirit is our helper.

37. What does the Holy Spirit help us do?

The Holy Spirit helps us obey God.
The Holy Spirit helps us serve others.

Elementary Scripture Memory Ideas

Making Scripture memory fun and easy will encourage your students to want to learn more. What a perfect time to hide His word in their hearts!

Try to vary your method—try new ones, and come up with your own. Let the kids invent a new method too! The more engaged the students are, the more likely they will memorize the Scripture verse.

Envelope Mix-Up

Put each picture and word of a memory verse on a separate piece of paper. Mix the pieces of paper and put them into an envelope. Make up enough envelopes to give one to each person or pair of people in your group. The first person or pair to put the words of the memory verse in the correct order is the winner.

Push Pin Review

Have each picture word of a memory verse written on a three-by-five-inch card or a piece of paper. Show the students the verse with the picture cards in order. Take the cards down and allow the students to reassemble the cards in order themselves. Try to allow each student to have a turn.

Make a Match

Create two sets of picture cards for each word (phrase) for the memory verse. Say the verse together as you show them the two sets of cards. Turn the cards over and have students take turns trying to find each picture word's match. When all matches have been found, say the verse together again.

To make this activity more challenging, write the verses incorrectly so that the group members have to correct the mistakes after matching the two halves of the card.

Whiteboard Erase

Draw the memory verse in pictures on the whiteboard. Have someone (or the entire group) "read" the verse. Then erase pictures one at a time. Have the class recite the verse again as though the picture was still there. Continue to do this until all of the pictures are gone, having the group say the entire verse from memory.

Hang-Man Memory

Draw a blank line for each letter in a memory verse. Ask one child to guess a letter. If that letter is in the verse, write it in the appropriate blank(s). Allow the student to keep guessing letters until he or she guesses incorrectly. You could modify this game by letting the group guess individual words. When they guess correctly, fill in the entire word wherever it appears in the verse. You might also write the verse reference on the board above the blanks for the verse or make the reference part of the puzzle. The first person to say the entire verse correctly wins.

Around-the-Table Memory

Have the group sit in a circle. Write the memory verse on a board where it can be easily seen. Assign one word of the memory verse to each person in the group. Then start at the beginning of the verse, and have each person say his or her assigned word in turn to complete the verse. Gradually increase speed so that the group must recite the verse faster and faster. At some point, remove the board so the group must recite the verse from memory.

A variation of this game is to have the first person in the circle say the first word of the verse, then have the second person say the first two words of the verse, and so on. Continue until someone repeats the entire verse from memory.

Create a Cheer

Turn the Scripture verse into a cheer. Have the children create a cheer from the words of the memory verse by adding motions, phrasing, repetition, and intonation that will turn "Go ye into all the world . . ." into a motivational cheer. Encourage creativity and movement.

Sing a Song

Many of us memorize words more quickly if we sing them. Turn the memory verse into a song by using a familiar tune. You can suggest a tune to a popular children's song or one that they have learned in church. Make it a chant, a rap, or a simple melody. Many verses have already been turned into songs or worship choruses

Prop-Up Memory

Use objects or props to represent key words or phrases that will help the kids remember. Connecting an every day object to a memory verse word will help them make a mental picture of the verse—a picture they can carry with them. You can select the props ahead of time, and let the kids help you "prop up" the memory verse. Or you can let the kids choose the objects and then search the church for them. They'll enjoy the search as well as putting it all together. The entire process will imprint the words, phrases, and meaning in their minds.

How to Lead a Child to Christ

As you present the lessons in this book, the opportunity will arise for you to ask the students if they have a personal relationship with Jesus Christ. If they do not, please carefully consider these suggestions.

1. Be sensitive to the leading of the Holy Spirit in the child's life.
Conversion is the work of the Holy Spirit. God will draw children to himself. Never force, coerce, or push children to make a decision. Salvation must be freely accepted. Be prepared for teachable moments.

2. Pray for the child.
Pray for open doors to share the gospel (Col. 4:2–4). Pray that God will prepare their hearts and make you sensitive to the opportunities.

3. Understand when the child is ready.
When a child understands that God is a being who loves him or her, when a child can know the difference between right and wrong, when he or she experiences sorrow for doing wrong, and when the child gains a basic understanding of Jesus as God's Son who died for his or her sin, then that child is ready to respond!

4. Know how to explain the plan of salvation.
Here is a method for presenting the gospel to children:

> Jesus wants children to come to Him (Mark 10:14–15).
> God loves you and sent Jesus to die for you (John 3:16).
> You have sinned against God (Rom. 3:23).
> The penalty for sin is death (Rom. 6:23).
> You can ask Jesus to take away your sins (Rom. 5:8).
> You can receive the forgiveness of sins (1 John 1:9).
> You can become a member of God's family (John 1:12).

5. Help the child pray to express faith in Christ.
Here is a simple prayer you might use: "Dear Jesus, I know I have sinned, and I am sorry. I turn away from my sins and ask You to forgive me. I believe You are God's Son and that You died for my sins. I confess my sins to You, and now

I want to receive You into my life as my friend and Savior. Thank You, Jesus. Amen."

6. Rejoice, review, and reaffirm. Celebrate with the child, and give them the opportunity to share with the whole group. Make sure the child's parents know about his or her decision. Encourage parents to read to them from the Bible daily and to model prayer and regular church attendance.

How to Teach Children to Pray

Children are very open, and their hearts are pure. Model childlike-faith prayers, be patient with childish requests and needs, encourage open, honest prayers, and allow children to grow through frequent and consistent prayer time.

Below are a few simple techniques to help vary your class prayer time and encourage students to directly participate.

Sentence Prayers

Have children take turns saying one-sentence prayers. A specific idea or topic can be suggested or left open-ended.

Circle Prayers

Have children hold hands and stand in a circle. Go around the circle, praying for the person on their right. (If they aren't comfortable praying out loud, they can squeeze the next person's hand to pass.)

One-Word Prayers

Begin with a sentence and allow children to fill in at random and out loud with one word. For example, you might say, "Jesus we thank You for . . ." or "Heavenly Father, help us this week to . . . ."

Prayer Requests

Allow a time of sharing needs, concerns, and requests. After each request, ask or assign a specific student to pray.

Open Prayer Time

Tell the students you are going to allow them to speak out if they would like to pray. Have everyone close their eyes. Wait for their responses, and then close in a final prayer.

Hands-On Prayers

If a student is having a specific struggle, serious illness, or situation, have the class gather around them, laying hands on them and praying out loud.

Partner Prayers or Small Group Prayers

If you have a large group of students, have them pair up or form small groups. Share requests and take turns praying for one another.

Silent Prayers

Introduce a specific need or prayer idea. Then give students a few moments of individual, silent prayer time before you or a selected student closes with an audible prayer.

Written Prayers

Create a prayer wall or board. Provide students with cards or notes on which to write their prayers, requests, or praises.

Modeling Prayer

Provide examples of prayers to your students by praying for them. Be conscious to make your prayers conversational—using language and verbiage the students would be comfortable using. Make sure you include praise, thanks, reflection, and requests.

Listening Prayers

Help students understand that prayer is not just talking to God but includes waiting and being still for Him to talk to us. Provide opportunities where students are quiet and still before God, allowing Him to speak to them.

Music Resources

A child's spiritual development must include opportunities to worship. Worship can include a variety of elements as we commune with God and He with us. Children's corporate worship should be done reverently, actively, and joyfully.

Typical elements of worship include prayer, bringing offerings, sharing praises, reading the Word, sharing a special song, a creative movement, drama, art, and music.

Below is a list of resources that can assist you in your worship through music:

- *Shout to the Lord*, Volumes 1, 2, 3, 4 by Integrity Music. Contemporary worship songs sung with and for kids.

- *iWORSHIP kids* by Integrity Music. High-energy worship music typical of Integrity's *iWorship* but recorded especially for kids.

- *Great Big Praise* Publisher, Lillenas Music.

- *Scripture Rock* by Provident Music. CD contains 50 Scripture verses set to a fun rock style.

- *Songs 4 Worship Kids* by Integrity. Multiple CD set includes many of today's popular worship songs and some new titles.

- *MOVE It Like This* by ZonderKidz CD and instructional DVD contain 10 songs from fast paced to slow and reverent for kids.

- *The Kids' Hymns Project* by Lillenas. Fifteen hymns arranged for children in an exciting, contemporary style.

Additional Resources

Discipleship

Now that I'm a Christian Bible Studies for Children by Donna Fillmore
Awesome Adventure by Through the Bible Publishers
Beyond Belief by Josh McDowell and Ron Luce
Raising Up Spiritual Champions by Gospel Light

Child Development

Child Sensitive Teaching by Karyn Henley
Postmodern Children's Ministry by Ivy Beckwith
Rock-Solid Kids by Larry Fowler
Transforming Children into Spiritual Champions by George Barna
The Faith of a Child by Art Murphy
Opening Your Child's Nine Learning Windows by Cheri Fuller
The Disconnected Generation by Josh McDowell
Teaching on Target by Group Publishing
Teaching with Heart by Jody Capehart
Is It a Lost Cause? Having the Heart of God for the Church's Children by Marva J. Dawn
Bringing Up Boys by Dr. James Dobson
Creative Teaching Methods by Marlene D. LeFever
The Five Love Languages of Children by Gary Chapman and Ross Campbell, M.D.

Instructional Aids

Sword Fighting by Karyn Henley
How to Study your Bible for Kids by Kay Arthur and Janna Arndt
The Big Book of Bible Skills by Gospel Light
Children's Ministry Resource Bible published by Child Evangelism Fellowship
Making Scripture Memory Fun by Group Publishing

801 Questions Kids Ask about God with Answers from the Bible by Focus on the Family

1001 Ways to Introduce Your Child to the Bible by Kathie Reimer

What the Bible Is All About for Young Explorers published by Gospel Light

Kidcordance Big Ideas from the Bible and Where to Find Them published by Zonderkidz

The NIVAdventure Bible published by Zonderkidz

KidsBible.com New Century Version published by Nelson Bibles for Kids

The Children's Worker's Encyclopedia of Bible-Teaching Ideas: Old Testament by Group

The Children's Worker's Encyclopedia of Bible-Teaching Ideas: New Testament by Group

The Really Big Book of Kids' Sermons and Object Talks by Gospel Light

The Encyclopedia of Bible Crafts for Children by Group

Reproducible
Activity Items

Lesson 1

Activity 2: *Comes down to one.* There are a lot of numbers in the Bible. This fun trivia exercise reminds students that all these numbers come down to the one God we serve. Also, can you name what books or stories in the Bible these numbers refer to?

_____ the redeemed in Revelation (Revelation 7:4)

_____ fed with loaves and fishes (Luke 9:14)

_____ years the Israelites spent in the wilderness (Numbers 14:33–34)

_____ days and nights of rain (Genesis 7:4)

_____ days Jesus spent in the wilderness (Mark 1:13)

_____ Jesus' disciples (Matthew 10:2–4)

_____ tribes of the sons of Israel (Genesis 35:22, Exodus 39:14)

_____ fruit of the Spirit (Galatians 5:22–23)

_____ churches in Revelation (Revelation 1:11)

_____ years Jacob worked for Leah (Genesis 29:18)

_____ years Jacob worked for Rachel (Genesis 29:27)

_____ days of Creation (Genesis 2:2)

_____ wings on the seraphs that Isaiah saw (Isaiah 6:2)

_____ days Jesus was in the tomb (Matthew 27:64)

_____ sons of Isaac (Genesis 25:24–26)

_____ God we serve!

Activity 2 Worksheet Answers:

144,000 of the redeemed in Revelation (Revelation 7:4)
5,000 fed with loaves and fishes (Luke 9:14)
40 years the Israelites spent in the wilderness (Numbers 14:33–34)
40 days and nights of rain (Genesis 7:4)
40 days Jesus spent in the wilderness (Mark 1:13)
12 Jesus' disciples (Matthew 10:2–4)
12 tribes of the sons of Israel (Genesis 35:22, Exodus 39:14)
9 fruit of the Spirit (Galatians 5:22–23)
7 churches in Revelation (Revelation 1:11)
7 years Jacob worked for Leah (Genesis 29:18)
7 years Jacob worked for Rachel (Genesis 29:27)
6 days of Creation (Genesis 2:2)
6 wings on the seraphs that Isaiah saw (Isaiah 6:2)
3 days Jesus was in the tomb (Matthew 27:64)
2 sons of Isaac (Genesis 25:24–26)
1 God we serve

Lesson 7

Activity 2: *Choral reading from Psalm 139.*

ALL: O Lᴏʀᴅ, you search me and you know me.

GROUP 1: You know when I sit and when I rise

GROUP 2: You know my thoughts from afar.

GROUP 1: You discern my going out and my lying down.

GROUP 2: You are familiar with all my ways.

ALL: Where can I go from your Spirit? Where can I run from your presence?

GROUP 1: If I go up the heavens, you are there;

GROUP 2: If I make my bed in the depths, you are there.

GROUP 1: If I settle on the far side of the sea,

GROUP 2: Even there your hand will guide me,

ALL: Search me, O God, and know my heart.

Lesson 10

Activity 2: *Worship word bank.*
Scripture is filled with words that help us learn about worship. Match the words below to the correct Scripture reference. Some Scripture may match up to more than one word, and some words may be used more than once.

teaching	assemble	responded	praise
flute	listen	come	read
voices	gather	dancing	cymbals
fellowship	tambourine	amen	message
read	book	make music	offering
prayer	suffering	bowed	
breaking of bread	sang	fellowship	

Match the words above to these Scripture verses.

Psalm 54:6	Nehemiah 8:5	Psalm 7:7	Isaiah 56:7
Exodus 15:20	Acts 15:31	1 John 1:7	Acts 2:42–43
Acts 4:24	Psalm 150:4–6	Psalm 149:3	
Psalm 96:8	Colossians 4:2	Deuteronomy 31:11	

Answers:
Acts 2:42–43—teaching, fellowship, breaking of bread, prayer
Exodus 15:20—tambourine, sang
Psalm 149:3—dancing, make music
Psalm 150:4–6 —praise, cymbals, flute
Deuteronomy 31:11—read, assemble, listen
Nehemiah 8:5—book, responded, amen, bowed
Acts 15:31—read, message
Acts 4:24—voices, prayer
Colossians 4:2—prayer
Psalm 7:7—gather
1 John 1:7—fellowship
Psalm 54:6—offering
Psalm 96:8—offering, come
Isaiah 56:7—prayer, offering

Lesson 20

Activity 2: *Unscramble.*
Part 1: Unscramble these words that describe Jesus.

1. TERAFH

2. SDEXIET

3. NIDVEI

4. RNAEUT

5. WREOP

6. TRIFS-RBON

7. ROLD

Answers:

1. FATHER
2. EXISTED
3. DIVINE
4 .NATURE
5 .POWER
6. FIRST-BORN
7. LORD

Lesson 22

Activity 1: *God and man*. Jesus did a lot of things that every human does, but He also did some things that He could only do because He is God. Decide whether the actions listed below show Jesus' humanity or His divinity.

	MAN	GOD
Went to a wedding		
Fed 5000 with loaves and fishes		
Ate with tax collectors and sinners		
Healed a blind man		
Forgave sin		
Raised Lazarus from the dead		
Blessed the children		
Slept on a boat		
Walked on water		
Asked for water		
Prayed		
Preached		
Rode a donkey		
Calmed a storm		
Cried		
Fished in the sea		
Fixed breakfast		
Wandered in the desert		
Was tempted		
Did not sin		

Lesson 33

Activity 3. Worksheet. What's in a name?

Names are very important for people in the Scripture. The names represented the families' experiences and hopes and beliefs about the future. Throughout history, new Christians would take a new name upon baptism. Some people even changed their names to represent experiences in their lives. Match these people's names to what their names mean.

David	God will strengthen	**Stephen**	God saves
Mary	hairy	**Leah**	fool
Ezekiel	bitterness	**Jesus**	a man
Ishmael	beloved	**Samuel**	God has heard
Naomi	my pleasantness	**Nabal**	Star
Esau	God hears	**Esther**	gift of Yahweh
Paul	God is judge	**Matthew**	gazelle
Daniel	small	**Andrew**	crown

These people's names actually changed after encountering God

Jacob	Usurper	**Abram**	Exalted Father
Israel	God's Defender	**Abraham**	Father of Many
Sarai	Princess	**Peter**	Rock
Sarah	Princess	**Simon**	flat-nosed

ANSWERS for "What's in a Name"

David	beloved
Jesus	God saves
Mary	bitterness
Samuel	God has heard
Esau	hairy
Paul	small
Nabal	Fool
Esther	Star
Stephen	crown
Matthew	gift of Yahweh
Andrew	a man
Daniel	God is judge
Ezekiel	God will strengthen
Ishmael	God hears
Leah	gazelle
Naomi	my pleasantness

Lesson 34

Activity 2. Worksheet. Proof of Life.
Decide whether these statements are true of the life Jesus talks about or whether they are false.
Look up the Scripture passages in John to help you compare and correct any false statements.

	True or False
1. He goes out into the darkness without a flashlight. John 1:4 (shines in the darkness)	
2. I read the Bible when I want to know how to live like Jesus. John 5:39-40 (the Scriptures testify about me)	
3. No one will believe me when I tell you this story. John 3:15 (everyone who believes in me)	
4. This water is a cesspool filled with mud and mosquitoes. John 4:14 (a spring of water)	
5. She watered the brown shriveled plant until it was green and growing again. John 5:21 and John 11:25. (raises the dead, the resurrection and the life)	
6. This street is a dead end. John 14:6 (the way and the truth and the life)	
7. We are hungry to hear about God. John 6:51 (the living bread)	
8. I keep everything a secret because I don't want anyone else to know. John 6:63 (the words I have spoken)	
9. He did not stop for anyone as they cried for help. John 10:11 (shepherd lays down his life)	

Answers:
1) F, 2) T, 3) F, 4) F, 5) T, 6) F, 7) T, 8) F, 9)

Lesson 36

Activity 1: *Missionary maze.* Pass through the cities and people that Paul visited on his missionary journeys. *(You will also need a map of Paul's journey)

[Start in] Antioch

Tarsus

Salamis

Jerusalem

Athens

Damascus

Caesarea

Laodicea

Corinth

Thessalonica

Philippi

Fair Havens

Syracuse

[End in] Rome

Lesson 40

Activity 2: *Abundance.*
We live in a world of plenty, but there are people in the world whose basic needs are not being met. This activity can help you see how much you need versus how much you have. Count how many of these items you have in your house. Then set aside that much money for a charity or mission fund. You may want to ask your entire family to participate in this activity.

Car	$.25 each
Rooms in your house	$.10 each
Dishwasher	$.25 each
Kitchen appliances	$.10 each
Canned goods	$.1 each
Telephone	$.10 each
Light bulbs	$.2 each
Winter coats	$.5 each
Shoes	$.2 each
Blankets	$.5 each
Television	$.25 each
Videos	$.10 each
VCR/DVD Players	$.25 each
Cd player/stereo	$.25 each
Personal computer	$.25 each
Toys	$.1 each

Lesson 45

Activity 2: *Fruit Jumble.* Unscramble these fruit of the spirit from Galatians 5:22-23. Then match them to their Scriptural definition.

OEVL	NEPTEACI	SEFAHLINSTUF
JYO	SIDKNSNE	TEESNENSGL
CAPEE	SODOSGEN	COLTSNROELF

[put the definitions in a picture of fruit]

Active grace	Happy in service	Sober
Deliverer	Moderation	Affection
Trustworthy	Well being	Endurance

Romans 5:3-5	Ephesians 6:16	Joshua 2:12, 14
1 Thessalonians 5:6	1 Corthians 13	2 Corinthians 10:1
Philippinas 4:4	1 Thessalonians 5:23	Ephesians 2:10

Answers to "Fruit Jumble"

Love,	Unselfish, affection	1 Corinthians 13
Joy,	Happy in service	Philippians 4:4
Peace	Well being	1 Thessalonians 5:23
Patience	Endurance	Romans 5:3-5
Kindness	Active grace	Joshua 2:12, 14
Goodness	Deliverer	Ephesians 2:10
Faithfulness	Trustworthy	Ephesians 6:16
Gentleness	Moderation	2 Corinthians 10:1
Self-control	Sober	1 Thessalonians 5:6

Lesson 51

Activity 1: *Word jumble*. Students unscramble the words in this puzzle and learn more about hope and courage.

Find hope and courage among these jumbled words.

GRNUEH   ___ ___ ___ ___ ___ ___

ERAF   ___ ___ ___ ___

SOLT   ___ ___ ___ ___

WOFADRR   ___ ___ ___ ___ ___ ___ ___

MOOVCREE   ___ ___ ___ ___ ___ ___ ___ ___

PELH   ___ ___ ___ ___

MGCION   ___ ___ ___ ___ ___ ___

IFHAT   ___ ___ ___ ___ ___

Unscramble the letters circled to form the three words below.

___ ___ ___ ___ ___   ___ ___ ___   ___ ___ ___ ___ ___ ___

Answers:
HUNGER
FEAR
LOST
FORWARD
OVERCOME
HELP
COMING
FAITH

Book of Common Prayer (1928)

Our Father, who art in heaven, Hallowed be thy Name. Thy kingdom come. Thy will be done, On earth as it is in heaven. Give us this day our daily bread. And forgive us our trespasses, As we forgive those who trespass against us. And lead us not into temptation, But deliver us from evil. For thine is the kingdom, and the power, and the glory, for ever and ever. Amen.

The Ten Commandments

Exodus 20:1-17 NIV

I. You shall have no other gods before me

II. You shall not make for yourself an idol

III. You shall not misuse the name of the Lord your God

IV. Remember the Sabbath day by keeping it holy

V. Honor your father and your mother

VI. You shall not murder

VII. You shall not commit adultery

VIII. You shall not steal

IX. You shall not give false testimony against your neighbor

X. You shall not covet

TEACHING CALENDAR

DATE	CONCEPT	SESSION ELEMENTS	ACTIVITY OPTIONS	TEACHING TOOLS

*See Step 4 in "How to Use This Book" – Create a Teaching Calendar